THE DYNAMIC *Duo*

THE HOLY SPIRIT & YOU

RICK RENNER

Charisma
HOUSE
Books about Spirit-Led Living

THE DYNAMIC DUO by Rick Renner
Published by Charisma House
Strang Communications Company
600 Rinehart Road
Lake Mary, FL 32746
www.charismahouse.com

Unless otherwise noted, all Scriptures quotations are from the King James Version of the Bible.

Scripture quotations marked AMP are from the Amplified Bible. Old Testament copyright © 1965, 1987 by the Zondervan Corporation. The Amplified New Testament copyright © 1954, 1958, 1987 by the Lockman Foundation. Used by permission.

Scripture quotations marked NKJV are from the New King James Version of the Bible. Copyright © 1979, 1980, 1982 by Thomas Nelson, Inc., publishers. Used by permission.

Phonetic pronunciations for Greek words are from *The New Strong's Exhaustive Concordance of the Bible.* Copyright © 1984 by Thomas Nelson Inc., publishers. Used by permission.

Library of Congress Catalog Number: 93-74605
International Standard Book Number: 0-88419-362-4

01 02 03 04 05   12 11 10 9 8 7
Printed in the United States of America

*I lovingly dedicate this book to all those whom
the Lord used to lead me to a fuller understanding
of the Holy Spirit.*

*I am eternally grateful to my parents,
Ronald and Erlita Renner, who taught me so well
to make Jesus Christ the Lord of my life;
to my aunt, Melita Davis, who prayed with me to
receive a new touch of the Spirit in 1974; and
to Kathryn Kuhlman, who demonstrated the
communion of the Holy Spirit to me for the first
time in that miracle service on the campus
of Oral Roberts University.*

*To all of these, I dedicate this book.
Thank you for allowing God to use you in
such a significant way in my life.*

CONTENTS

Section Four
The Responsibility of the Holy Spirit

Section Five
The Personality of the Holy Spirit

THE BOOK you hold in your hand right now holds the key to the mysteries of God, the power of God, the revelation of God's Word and the fellowship of the Holy Spirit.

It isn't so much *what* I have written in this book that will transform you, but about *whom* I have written. This book is about the Holy Spirit and you.

Most Christians live and die never knowing the fellowship and companionship of the Holy Spirit. They have heard about the Holy Spirit and may even know doctrinal answers regarding the Holy Spirit. But knowing *about* Him and personally *knowing*

Him in daily fellowship are two very different things.

Before there was a New Testament for the early church to turn to for direction, guidance and answers, they relied completely on the Holy Spirit. In those primitive years the church had power, miracles, healings, mass evangelism, apostles, prophets, evangelists, pastors, teachers and the gifts of the Spirit in amazing abundance. We all look back to that early time in admiration, wishing we could relive it in our own generation.

Today we are privileged to have not only the Holy Spirit but also the Word of God. This is the very best. Why then do we not see the same power and glory that the early church experienced? Why do we not see the power of the resurrection flowing in our midst?

While there may be many answers to these questions, it is certain that we have come to lean upon our own understanding, our own intellectual abilities — even upon the Bible — to such an extent that often we do not even consult the Holy Spirit for His guidance in our lives. We assume that we already know what the Holy Spirit wants to do. Because we do not lean upon Him the way the early church did, we miss opportunity after opportunity to see His power released before us.

There is no substitute for the Bible, but neither is there a substitute for the supernatural work of the Holy Spirit in the church. Remove the supernatural work of the Spirit, and all that is left is orthodoxy and religious works. Religious works will never raise the dead, cast out demons, heal the sick, or turn cities and nations to Jesus Christ.

In my own life and ministry I continue to learn how imperative it is for us to have intimacy and moment-by-moment communication with the Holy Spirit, no matter how knowledgeable we are of God's Word. If I had not cultivated a rich, solid relationship with the Holy Spirit through many years of traveling the United States and teaching the Bible, I would have been extremely skeptical and may even have disobeyed Him when He called me to move my family to the former U.S.S.R.

For the past two years we have lived in Latvia and traveled

throughout the former Soviet Union. There is no doubt in my mind or my family's that we would have perished many times without the help, guidance and comfort of the Holy Spirit. Furthermore, we have stood and watched in awe as His power has moved through our ministry to touch millions of people — saving them, healing them, performing miracles and delivering them from Satan's bondage.

The Holy Spirit has manifested Himself in ways we had only dreamed of in years past. In the short span of time since we arrived, He has enabled us to reach more than 150 million souls through a weekly television program, establish a church in the city of Riga, launch a Bible school to train leaders for all the churches which are springing up in that part of the world, and hold crusades and meetings in the various regions to build up the new local bodies of believers.

The key for me has been to learn to work with God's Word and to flow with the Holy Spirit simultaneously. The Holy Spirit never leads us contrary to the Word of God but rather confirms and supports it, as He is the One who inspired it (2 Timothy 3:16).

With the Bible in our hands and hearts and with an open spiritual ear to hear what the Spirit is saying, we should never fail. No people and no generation have ever been so blessed as those of us who live in this glorious church age.

I'm happy that you have picked up this book today. I believe this will be the start of a marvelous new adventure and spiritual journey for you.

All for which you have dreamed, all for which your heart has yearned, is in front of you. Read this book with an open heart and ask the heavenly Father to reveal the work of the Holy Spirit to you. *Your dreams are about to become reality.*

Rick Renner
Jelgava, Latvia

GETTING ACQUAINTED WITH THE HOLY SPIRIT

"The grace of the Lord Jesus Christ,
and the love of God, and the *communion*
of the Holy Spirit be with you all."

2 Corinthians 13:14, NKJV

ONE

THE
THIRD
DIMENSION

MANY YEARS ago, my heart began to search for a deeper walk with Christ. Surely there must be more to the Christian life than I was experiencing. It was as if there were a hole in the pit of my stomach, and I was yearning for God to fill it up with Himself. I searched here and there, looking for someone who could help me find this deeper place in God for which my heart longed.

I was raised as a Southern Baptist and had been saved at an early age. Living the Christian life was not new to me or my family. In my teenage years I ventured beyond our Southern Baptist church and was introduced to the power of the Holy Spirit in a marvelous way.

Yet now my heart longed for something deeper than an experience, something more lasting than an emotional high. I knew there had to be something more than what I had already discovered.

One day in the early 1970s, while flipping from one radio station to the next, I came across the most unusual program. It captivated my attention. It was a woman who was speaking about miracles and about a relationship with the Holy Spirit. It was Kathryn Kuhlman.

I sat in the kitchen by our radio, my ears glued to every word, as she described an ongoing, intimate relationship with the Holy Spirit. My heart nearly beat out of my chest. I was so excited to hear someone speak about that deeper place in God for which I so desperately longed.

Second Corinthians 13:14 was her text that day. She read, "The grace of the Lord Jesus Christ, and the love of God, and the communion of the Holy Spirit be with you all" (NKJV).

As I heard her speak from this Scripture passage, the phrase "the communion of the Holy Spirit be with you all" nearly jumped out at me! I was aghast that, after being a serious Christian for so many years, I had never noticed that last statement about the communion of the Holy Spirit.

The first part of the verse contained no new ideas for me at all. Of course not! I had grown up as a Southern Baptist. If there was anything I was well aware of, it was the grace and love of God.

Our doctrines were centered in the grace of God. I couldn't begin to count the times I had stood in front of the pews of our church and sung "Amazing Grace" or "Grace Greater Than Our Sin." Those songs, almost like New Testament Scripture, were etched into my heart and soul for the rest of my life. Even as I write at this moment, I can still hear our congregation belting out the words: "Grace, grace, God's grace, grace that will pardon and cleanse within. Grace,

grace, God's grace, grace that is greater than all our sin."

And, of course, we knew about the love of God. Even the smallest child in Sunday school knew about the love of God and could quote John 3:16 from memory: "For God so loved the world that he gave his only begotten son." God's unconditional love was the first thing we were taught in our spiritual upbringing in Sunday school, and as adults we placed it side by side with our emphasis on grace.

Our church emphasized God's grace and love, but we felt that looking to the Holy Spirit, even in the smallest way, somehow robbed Jesus of our full attention.

When Kathryn Kuhlman read this verse on the radio, that last statement dropped into my heart with a thud, and I wondered, "Why in the world haven't I ever noticed this statement before? What is the communion of the Holy Spirit? Is this what my heart is seeking for so desperately?"

Of course I had a relationship with God the Father. Every Christian has that relationship by virtue of the new birth. I knew I had a relationship with Jesus, God's Son. My relationship with Him was the reason that I was born again. But the idea of a real, living relationship with the Holy Spirit was totally foreign and a little scary to me. I didn't want to do something wrong or give attention to the Holy Spirit that I should be giving only to Jesus.

The word *communion* was an enigma to me also. To my mind it carried images of the grape juice and wafers that we used every quarter of the year when our church took communion. To me the word *communion* meant "the Lord's supper."

But it was obvious that this statement wasn't about the Lord's supper or grape juice and wafers. This word *communion* was speaking about a deep relationship with the Holy Spirit that I didn't have.

In the weeks to follow I tuned in to Kathryn Kuhlman's radio program daily. The more I listened to her, the more apparent it became that whatever this communion with the

Holy Spirit was, she had it. She spoke so naturally about the Holy Spirit and her relationship with Him. She spoke of Him as though He were a real person, a real friend with whom she shared her mornings, her afternoons and her evenings. She testified of miracles that occurred in services she held all over the United States, and every Friday actual excerpts of those miracle services were broadcast on her radio program.

A seed of obsessive curiosity dropped inside me, and I was determined to discover this deeper place in God that I was now hearing about from Kathryn Kuhlman.

Eventually everyone comes to a place of dissatisfaction in their spiritual lives. This is the place where new experience in God always begins. Jesus said, "Blessed are they which do hunger and thirst after righteousness: for they shall be filled" (Matthew 5:6).

They are "blessed" because this spiritual hungering and thirsting leads them down the path to encounter a new experience with God that will fill them. But the time of hunger and thirst that precedes this infilling is often one of the most miserable, unsatisfying periods one could ever pass through. Amazingly, it is this state of spiritual misery that drives us to a position where God can reveal Himself to us in a more meaningful, personal and powerful way.

Fellowship With God

First John 1:3 says, "That which we have seen and heard declare we unto you, that ye also may have fellowship with us: and truly our fellowship is with the Father, and with His Son Jesus Christ."

It made sense to me that if we could have fellowship with the Father and the Son, then we should also be able to have fellowship or communion with the Holy Spirit. Why would the Holy Spirit be exempt from this fellowship?

I had grown up hearing preachers, evangelists and Sunday school teachers asking people the question, Do you have a relationship with Jesus Christ? Because I had heard this question repeated so many times, I knew we were supposed to have a relationship with Jesus, and I had that relationship.

I had prayed to the Father and had sought to have fellowship with Him my whole life. But I thought the Holy Spirit was the mysterious part of God that we could never know or understand in a personal way. He was the invisible, intangible part of God that we believed in but never experienced apart from the conviction of sin when we were first saved or were in need of repentance. And, of course, we prayed for Him to help us as we went out every Wednesday night on Sunday school visitation. But that was the scope of my experience with the Holy Spirit.

Doctrinally and intellectually, I understood a lot about the work of the Holy Spirit. As good Southern Baptists we were taught the truth about Him working to produce the character of Christ and the fruit of the Spirit in us, conforming us into the image of Jesus Christ. That teaching was superb, but mainly mental, and it never put me in touch with the Spirit's power in a real way.

To my young mind, the Holy Spirit's work that we could actually *feel* was very limited. We only expected to feel the conviction of sin or to feel His presence in a song service.

According to Acts 1:8, I knew the Holy Spirit was supposed to give us power to be witnesses, but I had rarely, if ever, experienced that power as I sought to witness for Christ. Now, as I listened to Kathryn Kuhlman's radio program, I couldn't help but notice that this woman had a relationship with the Holy Spirit that I had never experienced.

I was completely mesmerized by what I was hearing. I had never heard anyone speak to the Holy Spirit in this way. I spoke to Jesus, and I spoke to my heavenly Father, relating to each of them intimately from my heart. Would it then be OK to relate to this third person of the trinity in the same way as this woman did?

Eagerly I started researching the Greek words used in 2 Corinthians 13:14. The Holy Spirit illuminated wonderful things to me which are not usually accessible to the reader who is unacquainted with the Greek language. Over the years this verse has continued to unfold and bring forth many precious truths to me. This book must begin with 2 Corinthians 13:14 because that is where my own deeper walk with the Spirit began in 1974.

TWO

A Picture
of Your
Spiritual Life

P AUL WROTE, "The grace of the Lord Jesus Christ, and the love of God, and the communion of the Holy Spirit be with you all" (2 Corinthians 13:14, NKJV).

As I took a closer look at this wonderful verse, I began to see that it was a picture, a snapshot if you will, of the spiritual development God desires for every Christian. The verse can be divided into three distinct parts:

1. the grace of the Lord Jesus Christ

2.   the love of God

3.   the communion of the Holy Spirit

The first phrase is "the grace of the Lord Jesus Christ." Those who are sure of their salvation know that their spiritual journey began with the grace of the Lord Jesus Christ. Without this marvelous grace we could not be born again and know God. Hence, the first part of this verse could be indicative of our first experience with the Lord. Paul refers to this first experience with the grace of God in Ephesians 2:8 when he says, "For by grace are ye saved."

Once this grace touches our lives, we are hurled forward into the second part of 2 Corinthians 13:14, which is indicative of our second phase of spiritual growth as a Christian — "the love of God." There is nothing with which to compare the love of God that a new believer experiences when he or she has just been saved.

At that glorious moment when the burden of sin rolls away, you really know you are loved by God. I have often heard new believers say that when they were born again they felt as if they had been baptized in divine love. It seemed so real at the moment that they were nearly able to reach out into the air and scoop it up with their hands.

This is one reason why it is such a joy to lead people to Christ. When brand-new Christians lift their heads and open their eyes, the look on their faces is worth more than all the money the world has to offer. Their faces gleam with joy because they know they are forgiven, cleansed, and that they are new creatures. Most of all, they know they are loved.

The problem is that this wonderful sense of love is so real and so life-changing that new and immature believers often try to reproduce that same feeling over and over again throughout the years to come. Rather than move forward in their spiritual growth, they get stuck on past emotions.

As I was growing up in our church, I distinctly remember

many young people trying to get "resaved" year after year at church camp. One poor girl made a public profession for Christ five times during those years. Back then I didn't understand why she kept going forward to receive Him again and again, but now I do.

During church camp, her heart was tender and sincerely set on the Lord. But after camp was over and she returned to the daily affairs of life, her emotions toward the Lord subsided. When church camp commenced again the next year, she realized that her heart was not as tender toward the Lord as it had been the year before, and so she questioned her salvation. This drove her to the altar again and again, trying to regain the feeling of God's love that she first experienced when she was truly born again.

I saw many adults do the same thing at our church's yearly revival meetings. A percentage of adults would always move to the front of the altar during the invitation to rededicate their lives or to seek assurance of their salvation. Though some of them genuinely needed to go forward, the majority were trying to regain what they had lost through the years — the feeling of God's love.

While we must never lose "the wonder of it all," neither must we seek to relive past experiences which were never intended to be relived over and over again. We must not stop our growth because we want to recapture the feelings we had when we were born again.

If you find yourself in this rut, it is probably past time for you to press ahead into another realm of spiritual development — "the communion of the Holy Spirit" (2 Corinthians 13:14). In this third phase you will come to know new power, new strength, new ability, new discernment and, yes, new and more mature spiritual emotions.

This spiritual maturity is the very thing for which your heart is yearning. In this third realm, you learn how to walk in the Spirit, move in the power of God, know the voice of God, have the mind of Christ, pray effectively, receive direction, be sensitive to Him and much more. This third realm is where spiritual maturity begins — and it is available to everyone. That is why Paul prayed for the communion of the Holy Spirit to "be with you all."

The grace of God is where all this begins, and the realization of God's love is the foundation for everything we do. But this communion with the Holy Spirit is a launching pad for a life of supernatural power and consistency of godly character. Without this daily communion with the Holy Spirit it is impossible to live a victorious Christian life.

If your heart is saying, "Surely there must be more to the Christian life than what I'm experiencing right now," welcome to the wonderful place of spiritual misery! God-ordained misery brings you to this third phase of spiritual growth.

Intimacy, Partnership and Responsibility

We must carefully consider the word *communion* to understand and enter into this deeper walk with the Holy Spirit. The word *communion* comes from the Greek word *koinonia* (koy-nohn-ee-ah), a very old Greek word that predates New Testament times.

Primarily, the word *koinonia* conveys three different ideas: 1) intimacy, 2) partnership and 3) responsibility.

First let's look at a verse of Scripture where the word *koinonia* illustrates this idea of intimacy. In Galatians 2:9 Paul describes his relationship with the apostolic brethren in Jerusalem. He tells us, "And when James, Cephas, and John, who seemed to be pillars, perceived the grace that was given unto me, they gave to me and Barnabas the right hands of fellowship [*koinonia*]."

The apostles had been together a long time and were cherished friends. Now they were inviting Paul to step into their intimate circle of friendship. From my own experience, I know that when leaders walk together for many years, share good times and bad times, and stick it out with each other, their friendships are very special. These relationships are so special that they often exclude others. This kind of friendship circle is very difficult to penetrate.

In addition to being long-standing friends, these men were apostles. They were not like other people. They had been with Jesus. They were entrusted with laying the foundation of the New Testament church and were well aware of their awesome responsibility. A newcomer would not easily jump into the middle of this circle. This circle belonged to the loyal, the committed, to those who were mature in God.

Their inviting Paul to join them was a great sign that they approved of him personally and respected the work of God in his life. When they gave him the right hand of fellowship, they were not inviting him over for small talk. Remember that this word *fellowship* is the word *koinonia,* which means they were opening the door for him to enter their sanctum of tender and intimate fellowship with one another. This was to be a relationship built on intimate and meaningful communion and based on absolute trust.

From this example and many others just like it, we know that the word *koinonia* can carry the idea of an intimate relationship. Since *koinonia* is used in 2 Corinthians 13:14 for *communion,* this means the verse could be translated, "...and the *intimacy* of the Holy Spirit be with you all."

The second meaning of the word *communion (koinonia)* is that of partnership. For example, a form of the word *koinonia* is used in Luke 5:7 after Jesus caused a miraculous catch of fish. Because Peter's boat was not sufficient to hold the whole catch, he called to other fishermen in a nearby boat to come and assist him. The verse says, "And they beckoned unto their *partners* which were in the other ship, that they should come and help them" (italics added).

I want you particularly to notice the word *partners* in this verse. This word *partners* is a form of the word *koinonia.* In this verse it speaks of real, legitimate business partners who are working together on the same job, for the same cause, as one team.

These partners were working with Peter every day and in fact may have even worked for Peter in his fishing business. Keeping this in mind, we could translate 2 Corinthians 13:14, "...and the *partnership* of the Holy Spirit be with you all."

Then we come to the third idea conveyed by the word *communion (koinonia)*. This third meaning is that of responsibility.

A good example of this can be found when Paul wrote to the Philippian church, commending them for their generosity. He said, "Notwithstanding ye have well done, that ye did communicate with my affliction" (Philippians 4:14). The word *communicate* is a translation of another use of the word *koinonia*.

At the time that Paul wrote the Philippian letter, he had been traveling and ministering to numerous churches. Of all the places where he had been going to preach, none cared for him financially the way they should. In order to cover his expenses, he was working as a tentmaker during the day and preaching and training leaders during the evenings. He was pouring his heart and soul into churches who were not financially helping to bear his load while he helped them.

In the midst of this stressful situation, Paul received a special delivery letter from the Philippian church. In that package he found a sizable offering which the Philippians had given to support him while he was out in the field ministering. While other churches were neglectful of their responsibility, the Philippian church was careful to remember Paul and his own natural needs.

In other words, the Philippian church didn't just say, "We'll pray for your situation, brother," and then forget about him. Instead, they understood their responsibility to help Paul do his job, so they took up an offering to support him and his ministry. They took responsibility for him.

Therefore 2 Corinthians 13:14 could also be translated to say,

"...and the *responsibility* of the Holy Spirit be with you all."

So the three "meanings" of the word *koinonia* carry three primary ideas for us.

The *intimacy* of the Holy Spirit be with you all.

The *partnership* of the Holy Spirit be with you all.

The *responsibility* of the Holy Spirit be with you all.

In later chapters of this book we'll look at some of the other things the Scriptures say about these three aspects of the Holy Spirit.

The Human Heart's Deepest Desire

Most believers long to know a deeper place in God. There are multitudes of Christians who really love God but have no joy because they have not experienced this deeper place in Him.

Striving to please God and to do what is right, they go to church week after week, wondering why they feel so power-less and empty as a Christian. But they faithfully keep up the pace, hoping that somehow, someday, it will all begin to click for them.

Meanwhile, they feel guilty about the way they feel and dare not share it with anyone else. They keep their frustra-tions to themselves and hang on to the hope that maybe someday it will all begin to make sense. If you have ever been in this place, you know there is nothing more miserable and defeating than to be a Christian, sincerely trying to live the Christian life, without really knowing the joy and power of the Holy Spirit.

That is why I have written this book. It is not a deep, scholarly book, but a book designed to lead spiritually hun-gry people into a new place in God — a secret place — a place that God has been waiting for you to find for a long, long time. It is the same place that the early Christians discovered and the reason they could have eruptions of joy, even in the midst of terribly dark hours of persecution.

How I thank God for "the grace of the Lord Jesus Christ and the love of God." Were it not for the grace of God, you and I would still be without God in our lives. And were it not for the love of God, the Lord Jesus Christ would never have hung on Calvary's cross for you and me, nor would you and I have a true sense of self-worth by knowing His unconditional love.

But now God is calling you onward to the third step — "the communion of the Holy Spirit."

Every believer eventually reaches this turning point, a time when the heart is no longer satisfied and seeks for more. It is then that God's Spirit beckons us to come closer, to come into a deeper place.

In the chapters to come you will see that during the days of Jesus' humanity on earth, He lived in this communion with the Holy Spirit. Jesus knew the intimacy, partnership and responsibility of the Holy Spirit, not merely as a mental doctrine, but as a constant, daily reality in His life. His relationship with the Holy Spirit was His source of power, His vehicle of divine revelation and His strength to cope with the throngs of people who came to Him for ministry.

If the cry of your heart is to walk as Jesus walked or to know the power of the Holy Spirit as the disciples did in the book of Acts, you have picked up the right book. Now read on and see how you too can come to know personally the intimacy, partnership and responsibility of the Holy Spirit.

A whole new realm of God awaits you!

GETTING
PAST THE
WEIRDNESS

IN THE early 1970s I ventured beyond the walls of my denominational church to find a more meaningful relationship with the Holy Spirit. I realized there was much more to the Holy Spirit than I had thought.

I laid aside all my previous thoughts about the gifts of the Spirit being passed away and tongues being wild emotionalism and decided to take an honest, open-minded look at the Word of God on these subjects. The day finally came when I realized I had been robbed of something wonderful God had planned for my life and for every believer.

While I was grateful for my good Southern Baptist up-bringing and the marvelous teaching I had received in my church, now I was ready to receive the missing ingredient I had been seeking. I was so spiritually hungry and thirsty that it didn't take but a moment for me to be completely filled with the Holy Spirit when I finally opened my heart.

After this, I decided I needed to make some friends who could help me grow in my relationship with the Holy Spirit. But the only group that seemed to know something about the supernatural power of the Holy Spirit was the Pentecostals, and I was afraid of them. I had heard stories about their wild meetings, snake handling, swinging on chandeliers and rolling in the aisles of churches.

In the Baptist church I grew up in, the kids even made fun of the way Pentecostal women looked. The men always seemed to have beautiful suits, but their poor wives looked as if they had been stored away in a closet and were only occasionally brought out for the public to see.

When we were young, the way Pentecostal girls dressed at school was also a big turn-off to me and my Baptist friends. They wore long sleeves, buttoned-up collars, dresses down to their ankles and beehive hairdos. I always wondered how they got so much hair to stand on top of their heads. I also wondered how long their hair would be if they took the beehive down. Surely it would drag the floor. On top of all that, those poor girls from the Pentecostal church never looked as if they had any joy. They looked very embarrassed, as if they felt like freaks. I felt sorry for them. That was my mental image of Pentecostals.

So when I began my search for people with a Pentecostal experience, I didn't want to find it among Pentecostals. That wasn't attractive to me at all. So I looked for a more refined kind of Pentecostal — charismatics. These were people from every denominational background who had received the in-filling of the Spirit as I had but were not like old-fashioned Pentecostals.

Back in those days there weren't as many large charismatic churches as there are today. Nevertheless, all over the nation charismatic believers were meeting together in small home Bible studies, listening to teaching tapes and learning to move in the gifts of the Holy Spirit. I located a group like that in our town, found out what time the next home meeting would begin and decided I would attend.

My anticipation for that first meeting grew every day. I had only dreamed of seeing the power of God as I read about in the book of Acts. Now, as the day for that meeting approached, my heart skipped a beat every time I thought about being with other believers who had also been filled with the Holy Spirit. I knew I was about to step into the book of Acts.

My First Experience at a Charismatic Meeting

Finally the day came. The meeting began at 7 P.M. Because I wanted to see what other Spirit-filled people were like, I decided to go early. I was excited and scared at the same time.

Because of everything I had heard from fellow Baptists about wild emotionalism, I was a little apprehensive. But I had been filled with the Spirit myself, so I knew it was a genuine experience.

I walked in, picked a seat, placed my Bible there and went to the kitchen to get a cup of coffee before the meeting started. Everyone looked very normal to me. They were doctors, nurses, teachers, housewives and lay preachers. They were very nice, very normal-looking people. When it was time for the meeting to begin, I returned to my seat full of expectation.

The meeting started quite normally with an opening prayer and a few testimonies. After that the little group sang praise choruses and then began to "sing in the Spirit." This was the first time I had ever heard anyone "sing in the Spirit." It was the most beautiful thing I had ever heard. It sounded as if the angels of heaven had descended into that room and were singing the praises of God with us. I was enraptured.

Suddenly, with no warning, the woman sitting in the chair next to me threw her body back in her chair and went rigid. I looked at her as she leaned down on the arms of her chair and pressed back and upward at the same time. She looked as if she had lapsed into some kind of trance!

In a high-pitched tone she started shrieking, "Oooh! Ooooooooooooh! Ooooooooooooooh!" Her eyelids fluttered and twitched. The veins in her neck were bulging. Her voice rose up and down, up and down, again and again.

I was shocked that no one else paid attention to what was happening. I didn't know if what she was experiencing was good or bad, so I leaned close and asked her softly, "Are you all right?"

She answered, "He's here! He's here! He's here right now!"

I couldn't figure out whom she was talking about. I didn't know how she could possibly know someone was there because her eyes were shut. I asked her, "Who's here?"

She gulped for a breath of air. Stammering to get the words out, she said, "He, He, He, He, He," and then finally she burst through her stuttering and proclaimed, "He's here! The Holy Spirit is heeeeeeeeeeeeeere!"

Adrenaline surged through my body upon hearing her announcement. This was what I had hoped to see — a supernatural manifestation of the Holy Spirit. I could hardly believe it! This was my first time with a group of charismatics, and I was already about to experience something powerful.

She started moaning again: "Oh, oh, oh, ooooooooooh."

I whispered to her, "Where is He? How do you know the Holy Spirit's power is here right now?"

As quick as a flash, her hands were unbuttoning the cuffs on her sleeves, and she rolled her sleeves up above her elbows. I watched in amazement, not knowing what she was doing. "There," she said. "Do you see those goose bumps on my arms? That is how I know the Holy Spirit's power is here right now! Those goose bumps are the witness of the Holy Ghost!"

I stared down at her arms and gazed as hard as I could. Sure enough, her arms were covered with tiny little chill bumps. I wondered why she thought those chill bumps were the witness of the Holy Spirit.

Never in my entire Christian life had I encountered Holy Spirit goose bumps in the Baptist church. Now my mind was reeling. Was this what the Baptists had warned me about all these years?

Still, because I was so hungry and wanted to believe so badly, I reached down, unbuttoned my cuffs and rolled up my sleeves to see what was happening to my arms. Sure enough, there they were — goose bumps. But I knew my goose bumps were due to the fact that the house was cold. My goose bumps were just goose bumps. There wasn't anything supernatural about the little bumps on my arms. A small adjustment to the thermostat, and they would go away.

Because no one else in the group seemed to think it strange, and because I was the newcomer to this Spirit-filled life, I decided they must all be right. But the whole thing seemed very strange to me. I walked away from that first meeting trying hard to believe I had encountered something wonderful and marvelous —— Holy Spirit goose bumps!

Strange as the lady in the chair next to me was, and as confused as I was by the goose bump ordeal, I couldn't get away from the presence and power of God I felt when we were singing in the Spirit. I knew that, even if nothing else had been real, what I had experienced during that worship was of God.

Charismatic Flippers

A short time after this I heard of a radio preacher from

another city who was coming to hold a series of meetings in Tulsa. Word was circulating around town that this man had great miracles and healings in his services.

I decided that this would be the perfect opportunity to convert some of my Baptist friends to the "deeper" life. My first convert would be my Baptist Sunday school teacher. So I told him about the meeting and invited him to join me. I knew if I could just get him to a meeting, he would leave gloriously filled with the Spirit of God. After a little coaxing, I convinced him to go.

Once again, my anticipation was at an all-time high. As we waited for the service to start, I kept looking over at my Baptist Sunday school teacher, thinking, "Buddy, you are going to see things today that you never have seen before!" Was that ever prophetic!

When the radio evangelist came to the platform, I couldn't believe my eyes. I had only heard the man on radio, so this was my first time to see him. What a shock it was to my Southern Baptist system.

He was dressed in a white tuxedo with a bright red carnation tucked into his lapel. His jet-black hair was puffed up ridiculously high and combed backward, and it looked as if he had used a whole can of hair spray to keep it in place. The heels of his shoes were so high that they almost looked liked ladies' high heels. Lavish gold jewelry hung from his wrists and several diamond rings adorned his fingers. And he carried the biggest white family Bible I'd ever seen.

I grimaced when I saw the look on my Sunday school teacher's face — horror was written all over it.

The traveling preacher introduced himself and welcomed everyone to the meeting. He walked back and forth on the stage while he spoke. With no warning whatsoever, he froze in one spot while he was talking. I watched in amazement as he threw his body into the wildest contortions. I didn't know the human body could go in so many directions at the same time. It was one of the freakiest things I had ever seen. He flipped his back this way, then that way and then this way again.

During the whole time he kept yelling, "There He gooooooooooooooes! There He gooooooooooooooooes! The Holy Ghost is running up and down my backbone! Whew! There He gooooooooooooooooes!"

I shook myself and shut my eyes, hoping I was just dreaming. But when I opened my eyes, things had gone from bad to worse. The speaker was still flopping back and forth on the stage, and by this time the whole crowd around us had moved into the same kind of frenzy. The lady seated in front of us was wearing a back brace, and I kept thinking, "If this poor woman keeps flopping back and forth with that back brace on, she is going to break her body in half!" One woman across the aisle from us fell on the floor in a spasm.

The whole scene disgusted me. Of all the meetings to bring a Baptist leader to, this was the worst. All my hopes of introducing him to a deep and meaningful walk with the Holy Spirit dissipated right in front of me as these sincere but emotion-driven believers "did their thing." I was so turned off by this episode that I found myself going back to the drawing board to rethink this whole charismatic business.

To Be or Not to Be, That Was the Question

As a Baptist I was taught to take authority over the flesh and over my emotions. We were rightly taught to be led by the Word of God and not by unpredictable emotions. We believed in sound doctrine, sound thinking and sensible living that would lead others to Christ.

Now I was beginning to understand why our denomination had dismissed this charismatic business.

I longed to move into a deeper place in God, but if this was it, I was disappointed. Surely there was more to the supernatural walk of the Spirit than what I was seeing in the various meetings I was attending. It seemed that charismatics were completely driven by emotions, goose bumps and chills down the spine.

I soon found myself in prayer, asking the same question Shakespeare's Hamlet asked: "To be or not to be?" I was at a crossroads. I had experienced a new realm of God when I was filled with the Holy Spirit, yet I was completely unable to identify or agree with what I was seeing in charismatic circles. I truly didn't know what to do.

"Shall I go on with these people whose spiritual lives appear to be no deeper than a goose bump, or shall I return to my denominational church, which lacks power but at least has a sound mind?"

Unfortunately, there are many denominational people who have wanted more of the Holy Spirit than they've experienced in their traditional churches. But because they have seen such craziness done in the name of the Holy Spirit, they have returned to their denominational churches disappointed, not knowing what else to do. It took great faith and resolve for them to step through the door of a charismatic meeting for the first time. The fact that they even came to such a service declares that they were hungry and searching for something more.

Many of them backed away afterward, thinking, "If this is what it's all about, I don't want anything to do with it." I can't help but wonder how many people have become frightened of the deeper things of God because they've seen some kind of emotional display by those who were Spirit-filled but not really Spirit-led.

In all fairness, it is true that when the power of the Spirit comes, strange things often happen. In my own meetings across the world I have seen God do very unusual things. Remember that when the Holy Spirit was poured out upon the church on the day of Pentecost, the disciples' behavior was so shocking that people assumed they were drunk!

I have seen such supernatural joy in meetings that people cannot stop laughing. It is the joy of the Holy Spirit, which is something you would probably never experience in a traditional church, yet it can be a real evidence of the Spirit's strong presence. We cannot dismiss or eliminate the possibility of spiritual expressions that are different from what we are accustomed to experiencing. God is God, and He may do as He pleases.

But, honestly, as a Bible teacher who has traveled millions of miles to teach in thousands of charismatic meetings, I can attest that a lot — though certainly not all — of what is called the work of the Holy Spirit is not His doing. It's just pure flesh. I could write a comical book on the things I have seen take place in church services.

In some circles these unrestrained actions of flesh have been tolerated for so long that they have become acceptable behavior and almost Pentecostal tradition. Still, we are advised in Scripture to be careful about our outward behavior and are commanded to judge our actions and attitudes to see if they are done in the right spirit and according to the Word of God.

For example, the Corinthian church was endowed with many spiritual gifts, perhaps more than any other church of New Testament times. Yet Paul warned them to guard against emotionalism and conduct that was out of order. This plainly tells us that it is possible to have real spiritual gifts operating among spiritually immature people. Paul did not tell them to abandon the gifts. Rather he encouraged them to pursue them, but to make sure everything they did was done "decently and in order" (1 Corinthians 14:40).

There is order to what the Holy Spirit does. The word *order* does not necessarily mean a preplanned program that eliminates the spontaneous move of the Spirit. Instead, the word *order* in the Greek text carries the idea of doing something in a gracious manner.

The most supernatural services can be conducted peacefully. Even a strong prophetic word can and should demonstrate the gracious character of the Holy Spirit. Remember,

God is a God of order (1 Corinthians 14:33).

Only a mature relationship with the Holy Spirit will help you discern and avoid silly, immature manifestations of the flesh.

There were, of course, stable people involved in the charismatic movement of the 1970s. That movement was a real outpouring of God's Spirit which spawned many of the worldwide ministries we know today. But at that time, many charismatics' spiritual lives seemed to depend on wild emotion or goose bumps or chills down the spine.

What really bothered me was that when those feelings disappeared, I saw these people despondent and depressed, as if the Holy Spirit had left them. As a result of this wrong impression, they ran from meeting to meeting, trying to get a feeling back again.

I had been taught not to base my relationship with the Lord on feelings. So to me they were the perfect picture of instability, which was a far cry from the deeper life I desired.

FOUR

THE
DYNAMIC
DUO

AGAIN I found myself switching back and forth from one radio channel to the next, hoping to find someone who could answer my questions, when I heard some beautiful piano music. Then the announcer came over the airwaves and said, "And here she is, that young lady you've been waiting for, Kathryn Kuhlman!"

I'll never forget the first words I heard her say: "Hello, there! And have you been waiting for me?" Though this was her usual way of addressing her listeners every day, it seemed as if this woman were speaking to me personally.

She continued, "Today I want to speak to you about the communion of the Holy Spirit."

Within just a few moments she related how she had grown up as a Baptist in Missouri. That sounded pretty wonderful to this Baptist from Oklahoma! As I sat and listened to her teaching, I realized that at last I had found the person I had been looking for to take me into a deeper walk with the Holy Spirit.

I was so mesmerized by this woman's teaching and the way she talked about the Holy Spirit that when she announced she would be having a miracle service in Tulsa, I knew I had to be there. A new hope stirred in my heart.

"Please Don't Let Them Be Disappointed"

The meeting was to be held at the Mabee Center Auditorium on the campus of Oral Roberts University. That Sunday I excused myself from our church's Sunday school a little early and drove across Tulsa to ORU to get ready for that afternoon's miracle service.

When I arrived, I couldn't believe my eyes. People were standing all around the massive Mabee Center. The streets and parking lots were jammed with buses and carloads of people who had driven hundreds, even thousands, of miles to get to this service.

I had never seen anything like it. I was grateful that a friend had coaxed me into singing in the Kathryn Kuhlman choir, because choir members were taken right into the auditorium through a back-door entrance so we could begin rehearsing for the service. As I made my way in, I wondered, "Why have all these people come from so far to hear this woman preach?" Later, I understood.

The entire back half of the auditorium's bottom floor had been partitioned off for the critically and terminally ill. A huge crowd was standing outside, but the ushers were allowing the invalids to come and take their places in that special area so they would not have to fight the crowds.

From where I sat I could see wheelchairs, oxygen tanks, IVs, crutches, doctors, nurses and scores of people who were lying on stretchers. It looked as if a whole hospital ward had been emptied and brought to the service. Some of the critically ill had been transported by family members, while others were so close to death that they had been brought in emergency ambulances.

One hour before the service began, the main doors to the auditorium were opened. The crowd rushed in as fast as their feet would carry them. It looked as if a sea of humanity had been released all at once. People scrambled here and there, each trying to get a good seat, as close to the front as possible.

Soon, because the auditorium was filled, people were diverted to an overflow room where they could watch the service by closed-circuit television. An air of excitement and faith flooded the auditorium.

I couldn't help but keep looking back where the wheelchairs and stretchers were. The people there were so sick. I knew that many of them were coming out of desperation. This was their last hope. I found myself praying quietly, "O Lord, please don't let them be disappointed today."

The ushers walked up and down the aisles offering little booklets which contained testimonies of those who had received medically confirmed miracles in other miracle services with Kathryn Kuhlman. I reached out and chose three of the booklets and read them as I waited for the choir director to come onstage.

What amazing testimonies they were! By the time I had finished reading that third little booklet, I could sense my faith rising to a place where it had never been before.

Miracles Really Do Happen!

Moments before the service began, a crusade spokesman

came to the microphone and announced that miracles had already occurred, even while people were sitting, just waiting for the service to commence. Once again I could feel my faith and the corporate faith of that massive congregation rise even higher. The expectation in that place was so strong it could have lifted the building right off its foundation.

Suddenly the choir director appeared before us, urging us to stand to our feet and get ready to sing. The huge throng of people stood with us as we sang and worshipped the Lord. Thousands of voices — Southern Baptists, Methodists, Catholics, Episcopalians, Presbyterians, Lutherans, Greek Orthodox, Pentecostals and charismatics — were all joining together in adoration and worship.

The whole crowd began to sing the words to the song "How Great Thou Art." As we did, Kathryn Kuhlman came out onto the stage to sing with us. It was my first time to see her. Dressed in a long, white gown, she moved back and forth on the stage. In her deep contralto voice she bellowed out, "Then sings my soul, my Savior God, to Thee; how great Thou art, how great Thou art...."*

When the music and instruments stopped, Kathryn Kuhlman welcomed the people and then led us as we all sang "Alleluia." I remember thinking, "This must be what heaven will be like."

After some more music, Kathryn Kuhlman approached the podium and said, "I'm just going to speak to you for a few minutes today."

One hour later the crowd was so engrossed in what she was saying that no one noticed how much time had passed. It was as though we had all been invited to view publicly a private, dynamic and intimate relationship between this woman and the Spirit of God.

Here was a human being carrying on an intimate relation-

---

* "How Great Thou Art" by Stuart K. Hine. Copyright © 1953. Renewed 1981 by Manna Music Inc., 35255 Brooten Rd., Pacific City, Oregon 97135. International copyright secured. All rights reserved. Used by permission.

ship with the Holy Spirit right in front of us. Though I had grown up in church all my life and had been saved as a young child, I had never seen, experienced or heard about what I was watching that day.

The sermon was fine, but watching this woman relate with the Holy Spirit was more dramatic and impacting than any sermon that could have been preached. This was the most moving thing I had ever seen in my whole life. It was wonderful beyond words.

Interrupting her own sermon, she moved across the stage and pointed her finger out toward a section of seats at the top of the auditorium and said, "Someone right up there has just received a miracle. Stand up and claim your miracle!"

A whirlwind of power passed through the auditorium. Miracles of healing happened here, there and everywhere. Soon people were lining up near the stage to testify to what had happened to their bodies. Wheelchairs were emptied, paralyzed people got up from their stretchers and walked, blind eyes were opened, deaf ears heard, and the dumb were now speaking.

For about three hours I watched in amazement at the supernatural power of God. Everything I had ever dreamed, everything I had ever wanted to believe in, was happening right before my eyes.

A Look at a Living Relationship

My questions about God's miracle-working power came to a grinding halt when I saw those wheelchairs emptied and people who were brought in on stretchers now walking, even running, from one end of the stage to the other. Soon the whole front of the auditorium and the aisles on the bottom floor were jammed with people who had come forward to give their lives to Christ.

What a meeting! Not only were there miracles of the body, but also miracles of salvation for the human spirit! All my

Baptist teaching about miracles no longer happening was stripped away by the end of that service. And no one could accuse Kathryn Kuhlman of taking glory for herself. No one got the glory that day except Jesus Christ.

But more than anything else, even more than the healings and miracles, I had seen a vibrant, intimate relationship between the Holy Spirit and a human being, something I had only dreamed was possible. How remarkable it was to watch her interface with the gifts of the Spirit and respond to the Holy Spirit's gracious, gentle leading. Surely God had brought me to this place to see the kind of relationship He wanted me to have with the Holy Spirit.

When the service was over, I looked at my watch and was shocked to see how late it was. As I was driving home from the meeting that day, one thing became very clear to me: This woman knew a place in God that I did not know. It wasn't her sermon or her style that produced that power. That power was a by-product, an overflow, a spillover from her daily relationship with the Holy Spirit.

I began to reason, "If it is possible for Kathryn Kuhlman to know the Holy Spirit in this way, then it is possible for me too, since God has declared that He is not a respecter of persons" (see Acts 10:34). That afternoon, my perspective of everything spiritual changed and came into clearer focus.

I had the strong foundation of the Word in my life because of my Southern Baptist upbringing. I also had received the infilling of the Holy Spirit. But now my heart and soul longed to move into the secret place I had witnessed that Sunday afternoon on the campus of Oral Roberts University. I wanted to know the communion of the Holy Spirit.

From that moment on my heart panted for more — for the Holy Spirit and me to become intimate, cherished friends. I longed for the Holy Spirit and me to become *the dynamic duo*.

THE INTIMACY
OF THE
HOLY SPIRIT

...and the *intimacy* of the Spirit be with you all.

2 Corinthians 13:14,
author's paraphrase

FIVE

GIVING THE SPIRIT FREEDOM TO WORK

THE HOLY Spirit is the great revealer and teacher, and without an intimate relationship with Him, we cannot have a deep spiritual relationship with God.

Too many Christians are familiar with the fact that they are supposed to have a tender relationship with their heavenly Father, and they know this is possible because of salvation through Jesus Christ, God's Son. But the Holy Spirit is the neglected member of the Godhead.

In effect, many of us come to a saving knowledge of Jesus

41

and then stop, never going on to the next step: the power of the Holy Spirit. Most of the church has missed this close, personal relationship with the Holy Spirit that Paul prayed for us to know.

Moreover, it makes perfect sense that we should have this kind of fellowship with the Holy Spirit. He is the One who convicts us that we need Christ, brings us to a place of repentance, then imparts faith to us so we can believe and be saved. After doing all of that, He miraculously comes to live in our hearts, quickening our inner man and giving new life to our previously dead spirits.

He is the One who reveals Jesus to us, who teaches us to glorify Jesus and who brings everything that Jesus said to our remembrance when we need it. According to Ephesians 1:14, He is the "down payment" of our full salvation, which we will one day experience in heaven.

He is the One who anoints us for service and empowers us to live the Christian life. He is the One who opens up the Word of God to our understanding so we can know God's thoughts and ways. And He is the One who gives us the strength and wisdom to obey what God's Word tells us to do.

There is no Christian life without the Holy Spirit. Remove the Holy Spirit, and all that is left is dead formalism and religious traditions. The Holy Spirit is the life-force of Christianity. He is the One who raised Jesus from the dead, and He is still the One who gives spiritual life to men today.

If, then, there is no Christian life without the power of the Holy Spirit, why is the Holy Spirit so ignored? Why is this third member of the trinity kept in a closet, so to speak, and treated so mysteriously that many people never take steps to know Him better?

Why do Christians not experience fellowship with Him? Why do people become reactionary when someone does try to move into a deeper realm where they can know and experience the Holy Spirit in a more intimate way?

And if this special communion with the Holy Spirit is so vital for our lives, we must ask: How can we enter into such a relationship with the Holy Spirit?

A Child's Commitment

I was reared in a good Christian home and was taught the Bible from an early age. Because of that, I recognized I was a sinner when I was very young. At age five I distinctly remember understanding the penalty for my sin; I knew that if I didn't commit my life to the Lord, I was destined for hell when I died.

Never underestimate the ability of young children to understand the truths of God's Word. One of the worst mistakes you can make is to tell your children they are too young to make a commitment to Jesus Christ. If God is dealing with their hearts, don't stop them!

Talk to them and make sure they really understand, and if they do, don't stand in their way. There is no need for them to wait until they are older to get saved. If the Holy Spirit is drawing their hearts right now, let them pray the prayer of salvation. The prophet Samuel was a small boy when he met the Lord (see 1 Samuel 3).

I remember being under the conviction of sin for months. Nightly my mother laid next to my side in bed, praying with me, making sure I really understood what salvation was all about. Finally, one Sunday morning during the invitation, I marched to the front of our church, took the pastor by the hand and told him I wanted to be saved.

That day I got down on my knees and gave my life to Jesus Christ in the simplest way I knew how. I can remember it so clearly. My parents came down from the choir loft and joined me as I stood to make my public profession for Christ. It was a real salvation experience.

Later that day our pastor came to visit me at home. He instructed me in water baptism, and that night I took my first step of obedience as a Christian and was baptized. When I stepped into the baptistry to be baptized, I was so small that the people sitting in the congregation couldn't see my head above the side wall!

Something Missing

As the years passed, I realized something vital was missing in my life. I felt an emptiness inside, as if something weren't complete. Now I understand that it was my own human spirit yearning for that next step: the infilling and power of the Holy Spirit. However, as I've already said, we didn't emphasize the Holy Spirit in our church, and we often made fun of those who did. Yet I knew something was missing. I just didn't know what it was.

As a result of this, I began to doubt my salvation. Inwardly I struggled, wondering if I were truly. Why did I feel so incomplete spiritually? I knew those doubts about my salvation had to be false, because my salvation experience was real to me. But after I finally received the infilling of the Holy Spirit, that empty place was filled, and the doubts were forever laid to rest.

Staying Away From Extremes

Doctrine was an important emphasis in our Southern Baptist church. Doctrinally, we knew what we believed, and we knew what we did not believe — especially when it came to the work of the Holy Spirit. Because we lived in Tulsa, which was the headquarters of the Oral Roberts Evangelistic Association, Oral Roberts often became the brunt of our jokes. I can even remember people calling him the "pope" of the charismatic movement and poking fun at his wife, Evelyn, when she broke Pentecostal tradition and got a haircut!

As the charismatic movement gained momentum in the

Tulsa area in the early 1970s, making fun of Oral Roberts increased. Many pastors took aim at "charismatic excesses," teaching for weeks on end about the errors of the Pentecostal and charismatic movements. Some of their points were valid, while others were just paranoia resulting from all the exposure and attention given to the errors and excesses.

The usual stand was that the Pentecostal and charismatic movements contained nothing more than emotionalism, and preachers like Oral Roberts were charlatans who took advantage of widows on Social Security and sick people who were desperate for help.

Because we wanted to guard ourselves from these charismatic "extremes" in Tulsa, our pastor regularly taught the New Testament doctrines about the Holy Spirit. When it came to his preaching about the inward work of the Spirit in our lives, no one could teach it better.

However, when it came to the gifts of the Spirit or speaking in tongues, that is where he, and thus we, drew the line. We sincerely believed that these manifestations of the Holy Spirit had ended with the death of the apostles. We believed that these gifts were only given at the beginning of the apostolic age to help establish the church. Then, once the church was established, these kinds of gifts were no longer needed and therefore ceased to exist.

This is why we were so suspicious of men like Oral Roberts. To our way of thinking, he must be faking something that no longer existed. Now I understand that Oral Roberts has been one of God's greatest instruments of renewal for our century. But at that time in my life, I questioned both the validity of his ministry and his integrity because of the teaching I had heard.

Our teaching was Bible-based but selective. As far as we were concerned, the conviction of sin and the power to witness were the only things you could experience when it came to the Holy Spirit. We believed in His convicting work because it was essential for salvation. If someone became emotional about his need to repent, that was all right. But this was the limit to emotionalism in our church.

I would often see preachers walk up and down the aisles of churches during invitations, pleading with people to give their lives to Christ. Often they would pray, "Holy Spirit, I ask you to visit every lost man, woman, boy and girl with restlessness and sleepless nights until they come to Christ!"

As a young boy, this was very mystical to me. I could almost see the Holy Spirit following them home and keeping them up all night long. Finally, after many restless and sleepless nights, my childish mind envisioned them surrendering to this "hound of heaven" who had hunted them down.

During the invitation, we knew when the Spirit's convicting power fell on us because our hearts nearly beat out of our chests. That was a sure-fire way to know you were in sin! We really *believed* in this essential work of the Spirit in our lives.

Then there were all those soul-winning seminars! Any good Baptist, early in his experience, is taught to memorize Acts 1:8: "But ye shall receive power, after that the Holy Ghost is come upon you: and ye shall be witnesses unto me."

We intended to be the best witnesses in the whole world. The problem was that we wanted the power to witness, but we didn't want the Holy Spirit giving us an Acts 2:1-4 experience. It was almost like saying, "Yes, I want the Spirit's power, but...."

For me, it made Wednesday night visitation the biggest drag in the world. As we got in the car to begin our visits I would pray silently, "God, please don't let anyone be home tonight," or, "Lord, please let a big German shepherd be in the yard so we don't have to witness to someone tonight."

I hated witnessing. But I knew I was supposed to do it, so I went from door to door with the greatest frustration, always breathing a huge sigh of relief when our duty was done until the next week.

The Holy Spirit was a mystery. He was that part of God I could not really know and about whom I should not ask too many questions. He was basically off-limits except for these basic areas where we allowed Him to work in our midst.

Theologically, we knew He was the power of God who gave us the new birth and produced the character of Christ in us. But we would certainly *never* talk to Him. Why, it would be near blasphemy to attempt a relationship with Him!

The Value of Denominational People

As I told you in chapter 3, after I received a new touch of the Holy Spirit in my own life, I began to visit charismatic meetings in search of someone who could lead me into the deeper things of the Spirit.

I got the biggest shock of my life in those early days. I couldn't imagine intelligent people doing the silly things I saw and actually believing it was the Holy Spirit. Eventually in my search I found many well-balanced Spirit-filled believers, but those first years were traumatic.

I was from a background where we used our minds and diligently studied the Scripture. Now I found myself among people who were led by goose bumps and chills down the spine. I began to wonder if they had any brains at all. I am certain this is why many denominational people return to their former churches and never stick it out in charismatic churches. They get "freaked out" by some of the crazy things they see and hear and run back to where they came from.

This is unfortunate, for when the Holy Spirit's power is released in our lives, it should make us sound, sharp and highly intelligent people. The Holy Spirit is the *enlightening* ability of God.

Denominational people who visit Spirit-filled churches do so because they are seeking more of the Lord in their lives. They consider the possibility of visiting a Spirit-filled church for months on end before they really do it. Finally they get up the nerve to skip one of their own church services (which they rarely ever miss!) to visit one of those "other" kinds of churches. They want a fresh touch of the Spirit and come with a pure heart and a motivation to know God more intimately.

These are the kinds of people that charismatic churches really need. Denominational people are usually faithful and committed. The churches from which they come may lack power, but no one can question their stability. Denominational people are so committed that you can barely pry them loose from their churches, even when they know they are in a dying situation.

Some denominational churches have sat on the same street corner for 150 years and have had generations of families committed to them. Charismatic churches, on the other hand, spring up quickly and often disappear just as quickly. There are a few things that charismatic believers should learn from denominational people — and one of those things is stability.

When you've attended a stable, denominational church your whole life, and then you decide to visit a charismatic-style church that meets in the storefront of a local shopping center, the scene doesn't look very stable or inviting.

Let's face it: That is where most charismatic congregations begin. Even when they grow large, most charismatic churches meet in warehouse-type structures rather than religious-looking buildings with steeples. There is nothing wrong with that, and it is probably a better use of God's money and square footage, but it is a whole new arena for a denominational churchgoer.

It's a huge step of faith for people like that to step through those doors for the first time. That is why it is so sad when they come and observe freakish behavior as I did. We all know people who got so scared that they thought their only alternative was to go back where they came from and affect their dead church with the life of the Spirit. But rarely does a Spirit-filled believer change a denominational church.

For this reason, we need to avoid the "weirdness" that does not come from the Holy Spirit. Rather than trying to create fantastic shows of power, we must turn our attention to something deeper, more mature and more lasting. We must seek the fellowship and communion of the Holy Spirit first in our lives.

An earnest longing for mature fellowship with the Spirit of God will put an end to all the nonsense because a mature relationship with the Holy Spirit brings stability. He causes maturity to come as He works in our hearts and souls and renews our thinking by the Word of God. He doesn't come only to impart feelings, but to make us strong, stable and dependable.

There are times when you may feel the awesome sense of His power. I couldn't begin to count the times when the Spirit came so heavily upon me that my body was covered with chills from top to bottom. I'm sure my hair was standing on end. It is always overwhelming to experience such power.

There are unique encounters with the Spirit of God throughout Scripture, and, in light of this, we should give the Holy Spirit freedom to work in our midst in any way He desires. But we should never seek feelings or base our relationship with the Holy Spirit on feelings.

If you base your relationship with the Holy Spirit on feelings alone, when the feelings disappear you'll assume the Holy Spirit has disappeared too. The Holy Spirit is not a feeling. His presence may give you feelings from time to time, but do not confuse who He is with the feelings you may get from being in His presence.

My relationship with my wife works the same way. I love my wife very much, and sometimes I love her so much I get goose bumps just thinking about her. But if we have a conflict and those goose bumps disappear, it does not change the fact that I am still married to her, still deeply committed to her and still in love with her. Our relationship is based on trust, commitment and relationship, not on emotions alone. Thank God for the emotions, but they are the fruit and not the foundation of our relationship.

In the book of John, Jesus made it absolutely clear that the Holy Spirit is not a feeling because the Holy Spirit is not an "it." In the next chapter we'll look closely at how Jesus described the nature of the Holy Spirit.

SIX

An Intimate, Personal Relationship

WHEN REFERRING to the Holy Spirit, Jesus always used a personal pronoun. He called the Holy Spirit "He, Him" or "Himself" and never once referred to the Holy Spirit as "it" or "a feeling" (see John 14–16). He never even called the Holy Spirit "the anointing."

Jesus referred to the Holy Spirit with a personal pronoun because He related to the Holy Spirit as a real person rather than an invisible, intangible, mysterious, unknown quantity. For instance, in John 14:26 Jesus said, "But the Comforter,

51

which is the Holy Ghost, whom the Father will send in my name, *he* shall teach you all things" (italics added).

Notice that Jesus calls the Holy Spirit "He" in this verse. And that's not all. In John 14–16 Jesus calls the Holy Spirit "He," "Him" or "Himself" nineteen times (see John 14:16-17,26; 15:26; 16:7-8,13-15).

Why is this so important?

Because it tells us the Holy Spirit has assumed the attributes of human personality. Because He took on these human attributes, we are able to relate to Him personally. If He were an "it," it would be difficult to develop a relationship with Him. He has come down to our level and taken on traits we can understand so that we may know Him, relate to Him, cooperate with Him and have fellowship with Him.

What kind of human traits has He assumed? Nearly all of them, except those of a sinful nature. The Holy Spirit has and gives joy (Acts 8:8; Galatians 5:22) and love (Galatians 5:22) and experiences sorrow (Ephesians 4:30). And in John 14, 15 and 16 He does a myriad of things that any person would do. You will see more of these in section 3 of this book.

No one knew the Holy Spirit better than Jesus. Jesus was with Him before the creation of the world; He was with Him at the creation of the universe; He was conceived by Him in the womb of the virgin Mary; He was baptized by Him at the Jordan River; He was empowered to minister by Him; He was crucified in the power of the Spirit; and He was raised from the dead by His power.

Once Jesus was raised from the dead and ascended on high, the first thing He did was to give the promise of the Holy Spirit and pour Him out on the early church. Jesus knew the Holy Spirit inside and out and related to Him in a personal manner.

It is critical for us to understand that the Holy Spirit has the attributes of personality. These attributes are the basis for all fellowship and relationship we will have with Him.

Let me go back to the illustration of my relationship with my wife. I am married to a person, not an it. If I were married to an it, even though we were legally bound to one another, we would not know fellowship with each other. But because my wife is a person, I am able to talk to her, spend time with her and get to know her better every day. Often she and I set aside time for just the two of us. We are able to talk, share our deepest thoughts with each other or just be together. I have a relationship with her.

It is the same with the Holy Spirit. Though He is the invisible part of God, Jesus referred to the Holy Spirit as "Him." Since the Holy Spirit has the attributes of personality, it is possible for us to talk to Him, love Him, spend time with Him and share our deepest thoughts with Him. He, in turn, shares beautiful revelation from the Word of God with us. We can experience His joy, His love and, if we have grieved Him, His sorrow.

The early church knew the personality of the Spirit so well that when they needed to make a crucial decision regarding the gentile converts, they said, "For it seemed good to the Holy Spirit, and to us, to lay upon you no greater burden than these necessary things" (Acts 15:28, NKJV).

They knew the Holy Spirit so well that even if they didn't receive a specific word from Him, they were able to make necessary decisions because they personally knew what "seemed good" to the Holy Spirit. They knew what He liked, and they knew what He didn't like. They knew what "seemed good" to Him because they had more than an intellectual knowledge of Him. They shared a real communion with Him.

When you know someone well, like your wife or husband, you needn't always ask them what they think. Sometimes you already know what they think! You can tell simply by looking at them. You've walked with them long enough to learn their personality and their responses to different situations.

If I get upset, my wife knows it without my telling her because she knows me. If I get excited about something, I don't have to tell her because she knows me well enough to know when I am excited. She knows me because she has spent time with me, lived with me, talked with me, prayed with me. She knows me better than anyone else. Likewise, I know her.

We recognize human relationships easily because we can see our fellow human beings with our eyes and touch them with our hands. Naturally, these relationships seem more tangible to us than our relationship with the Holy Spirit because He is invisible to the eyes and impossible to touch with the hands. Nevertheless, knowing Him and His personality is just as real.

We must make it the highest priority in our lives to know Him the way that Jesus knew Him. The early church knew the Holy Spirit in this deeply personal way.

Developing the Divine Romance

To know the Holy Spirit more intimately, we cannot ignore what Jesus said in Matthew 6:6: "But thou, when thou prayest, enter into thy closet, and when thou hast shut thy door, pray to thy Father which is in secret; and thy Father which seeth in secret shall reward thee openly."

What did Jesus mean when He said to "enter into thy closet"? Was He actually telling us to get up every morning, open the closet door, shove all our shoes and clothes to the side, crawl inside that dark room, shut the door and pray? Of course not!

The word *closet* is taken from the Greek word *tameion* (tam-i-on), an old word that was first used to describe a secret place where one would hide his or her most valuable possessions. What would you do with a room like that? You would keep it under lock and key. You wouldn't leave a room like that open because people would traffic through

54

your most valuable possessions, and your things would be defiled.

As time progressed, the word *tameion* came to mean a place where you could put your money or treasure, knowing it would be safe there. In a certain sense, the word describes something like a safety deposit box at the bank.

By the time of the New Testament, however, the word *tameion* was used to describe a bedroom. A bedroom is a secret place where a treasured relationship takes place between a husband and wife. Their most intimate moments are shared only with each other, behind closed doors. You could actually translate this verse to say, "When thou prayest, enter into thy bedchamber."

Jesus uses the word *tameion* to convey the idea of intimacy with the Holy Spirit. Symbolically He is saying, "Just as a husband and wife enter into their bedroom and shut the door so they can bare their hearts and souls to each other in intimacy, so also you should have a relationship with God that is so tender, so special, so intimate, that it is shared only between you and Him and no one else."

Jesus describes prayer as something so precious, so private, it should occur in a bedroom with the door shut. This, of course, does not literally mean you must pray in the bedroom. The concept of a bedroom is only used to convey the idea of a single, isolated and solitary place. Jesus was telling us the proper attitude and environment for prayer.

When we enter into prayer, it should be done at a place and time when we are not interrupted, when the Holy Spirit can speak to our hearts and we can bare our hearts to Him — a sweet mingling together of human spirit with divine Spirit in holy communion.

Our daily priority should be to have this special time of communion with the Godhead through the Holy Spirit. It doesn't matter where we do this, but it should be private. During this special time each day, we must put everything else aside and concentrate only on Him. This is a sacred time.

The Gospels record that Jesus prayed early in the morning when the other disciples were sleeping, often out on a mountaintop or in the wilderness. There was nothing holy about the early morning hours or about praying on a mountaintop. But in those early morning hours Jesus found solitude and quietness with God, and on those mountaintops He could pray without the interference of others.

Your quiet place may be in your car when you are driving to work alone every morning. It may be early in the morning when everyone else in the house is still sleeping. Perhaps it is late at night after others have gone to bed. The point is that we must have a quiet place and time when we give ourselves wholly to the fellowship of the Holy Spirit.

People say, "Yes, I know I need to spend quality time with the Lord, but my schedule is so busy it's hard for me to find a time to do it." Be honest! You make time for what is important to you.

Do you have time to read the newspaper? Do you have time to watch the news? Do you have time to go to the movies? Do you have time for recreation? We always make time for those things that are important to us. If you really wish to have an intimate, personal relationship with the Holy Spirit, you will make time for it. It must become a priority as a matter of choice.

A Matter of Choice

My wife and I have traveled and taught the Bible together for years. When our children were very young, finding a quiet place to pray and study was always a challenge. When we arrived at our hotel room, the children were always so eager to get out of the car that it seemed as if they turned the hotel room inside out within five minutes. They were typical energetic little boys who were tired of driving in a car for hours at a time. While we were putting the room back together on one side, they were taking it apart again on the other side!

After breakfast it was time to put the little ones down for a nap. Then we would have a meeting with the pastor at eleven o'clock, and after that we went to lunch. Then it was time to put the children down for another nap. While they were sleeping, we would study and prepare for the evening service. By this time we were so worn out from everything that we would try to get some rest ourselves.

By the end of the meeting each night, we would eat a late-night dinner and fall into bed, hoping the children would sleep through the night with no problems. We became desperate for a quiet time with the Lord.

We tried getting up early, but it had to be *very* early because young children rise with the sun. We would take turns using the hotel bathroom as our prayer closet. Half the time we prayed so quietly to keep from waking the children that we wondered if God could hear us! When we tried to pray with authority against the attacks of Satan in our lives, our prayers were so soft and quiet we sounded as if we were whispering at the devil.

Finally, we made a difficult decision. We made a commitment to make the Holy Spirit the chief priority in our lives. It required us to make very difficult schedule changes in our preaching itinerary that were hard to bear. But by making these changes, both of us would be able to have daily, quality time with the Lord.

Since then our schedule hasn't changed much. We are still busy, still preaching around the world, still privileged to have three wonderful boys and still moving at the speed of light! After all these years, we still have to decide to set aside time to be with the Lord, or it just doesn't happen. We make time to do what we want to do in life. If it's important to you, you'll find time for it.

Our relationship with the Holy Spirit is the most important relationship in this world. I have learned that if my relationship with Him is strong, it makes my relationship with my wife and children good and strong. On the other hand, if I don't spend time communing with the Holy Spirit, it affects all my other relationships. I have learned that apart from Him, I truly have nothing to offer.

I have also learned that when I am in close fellowship with the Holy Spirit, He compensates for weaknesses in my life. In the next chapter we'll see how the Holy Spirit did this in the life of Jesus as well.

SEVEN

THE SECRET
TO SUSTAINING
STRENGTH

I HAVE often wondered, "How did Jesus have the physical strength to minister to multitudes of people without physically collapsing from the stress and pressure of it all?"

Jesus started His mornings in prayer, where He could gain and sustain the physical and spiritual strength He needed to minister to the masses.

This kind of sustaining strength was also evident in the apostle Paul's life. He faced grueling ordeals yet never seemed to wane in strength as he faced each trial bravely

59

and victoriously. What was the secret to this sustaining power?

Paul gives us the answer in Philippians 1:19. In response to all the problems that were facing him, he answered, "For I know that this shall turn to my salvation through your prayer, and the supply of the Spirit of Jesus Christ."

The phrase "the supply of the Spirit of Jesus Christ" is one of the keys to Paul's unbroken strength. The word *supply* is taken from the Greek word *epichoregeo* (ep-ee-khor-ayg-ee-o). It is a very ancient word that literally means "on behalf of the choir." The first part of the word, *epi,* means "on behalf of," and the second part of the word, *choregeo,* is the Greek word for a choir or a choral presentation. It is where we get the word *choreography.* What an important word this is for us to understand.

Let me explain it to you in greater detail. Thousands of years ago in classical Greece, a huge choral and dramatic company had practiced for an important theatrical performance. After putting in all their effort, time and energy, it was time for the show to go on the road. But there was one major problem: They ran out of money.

Though they had given their lives to this production and committed themselves to see it succeed, the show was over because they ran out of financing — it was all washed up for them.

Have you ever felt that way? Have you ever given yourself to something so completely that you didn't feel you had any more to give? Have you ever committed yourself to so much, so deeply, that in the end you didn't feel you had enough human strength to carry out your commitment, even though your desire was to fulfill it?

We all come to a place in our spiritual lives when we seem to have no more to give. We begin to wane physically and mentally. Even people with good intentions and a strong desire eventually come to one of these dead ends in their lives.

That is what happened to the choir in this story; they had come to this very place. No funds meant no show. It seemed that all of that energy, practice and commitment had been expended in vain. From all natural appearances it was the end of their dream. In reality, this dead-end place in their lives was the beginning of victory.

At that moment of despair, a wealthy man stepped into their lives. He had heard about their commitment. He had heard about how they had worked on this project for so long. And, because he was so impressed with their dedication, this wealthy man stepped in and made a sizable contribution "on behalf of the choir."

In fact, this financial contribution was far more than they needed. It was far more than they knew how to spend. It was an excessive amount.

And this is where we get the word *supply* in Philippians 1:19: "For I know that this shall turn to my salvation through your prayer, and the supply of the Spirit of Jesus Christ."

When you have given your all and you don't seem to have any more to give, that is when Jesus Christ steps into your life to make an overwhelming contribution of the Spirit's grace and power on your behalf.

Time to Receive

You may have come to a dead end in some personal area of your life. That, however, is usually the moment we really learn how to live. When we have no more to give, Jesus Christ — through the ministry and power of the Holy Spirit — picks up where we left off and makes an overwhelming contribution of the Spirit on our behalf. He paves the way to finish what He started in you.

The Word says, "Being confident of this very thing, that he which hath begun a good work in you will perform it until the day of Jesus Christ" (Philippians 1:6).

The problem with most Christians is that they lack quality

time with the Lord, a time when they can receive this divine infusion of power. If you will make time to fellowship with Him and allow the Holy Spirit to become your cherished partner and friend, He will fill you with the strength you need right now.

This is why your daily time with the Lord is so vital. You must learn how to have fellowship with the Holy Spirit so that this power will work in you and through you, sustaining you through the most difficult of times.

But if the Holy Spirit is an "it" to you, just the invisible, unknowable part of God — if He is just a feeling or goose bump or chill down the spine — it will be difficult, if not impossible, to enjoy His partnership in your life.

In the next section we will see how to develop your fellowship with the Holy Spirit so that He becomes your trusted partner. When this basic truth is established in your life, you will experience supernatural living in the power of God!

THE PARTNERSHIP OF THE HOLY SPIRIT

...and the *partnership* of the Spirit be with you all.

2 Corinthians 13:14,
author's paraphrase

EIGHT

JESUS MADE A PROMISE

A S WE have seen, the word *communion* in 2 Corinthians 13:14 comes from the Greek word *koinonia*, and it conveys the ideas of intimacy, partnership and responsibility. Let's examine the "partnership" aspect of the Holy Spirit.

If anyone understood the partnership of the Holy Spirit, it was the Lord Jesus Christ. Jesus' earthly ministry was completely dependent upon the Holy Spirit. From His birth, nothing that happened to Him and nothing that He did was apart from the power of the Holy Spirit. Moreover, the first thing

He did when He sat down at the Father's right hand in heaven was to send believers the gift of the Holy Spirit.

The ministry of Jesus and the ministry of the Holy Spirit are inseparable.

Consider these important facts about Jesus and the Holy Spirit:

- Jesus was conceived by the Holy Spirit in the womb of the virgin Mary (Matthew 1:18,20; Luke 1:35).

- Jesus' conception in Mary's womb was confirmed by Elizabeth, Mary's cousin, when she was filled with the Holy Spirit (Luke 1:41-45).

- Jesus' dedication as a baby in the temple was accompanied by the supernatural manifestation of the Holy Spirit as Simeon, the priest, and Anna, the prophetess, prophesied over Him (Luke 2:25-38).

- Jesus' arrival to Israel was announced by John the Baptist, who, under the anointing of the Holy Spirit, declared that Jesus was the One who would baptize in the Holy Spirit and with fire (Matthew 3:11; Luke 3:16; John 1:33; Acts 11:16).

- Jesus spoke of the baptism in the Holy Spirit and commanded His disciples to stay in Jerusalem until they had received this special endowment of power (Luke 24:49; Acts 1:4-5).

- Jesus was empowered by the Holy Spirit at the Jordan River when He was baptized by John the Baptist (Matthew 3:16; Mark 1:10; Luke 3:22; John 1:32).

- Jesus was given the fullness of the Spirit without measure (John 3:34).

- Jesus was led by the Holy Spirit (Matthew 4:1; Mark 1:12; Luke 4:1).

- Jesus returned from the wilderness in the power of the Holy Spirit (Luke 4:14).

- Jesus stated publicly that His ministry was a result of the power of the Holy Spirit (Luke 4:18).

- Jesus warned about the danger of blaspheming the Holy Spirit (Matthew 12:31-32; Mark 3:28-29; Luke 12:10).

- Jesus taught about the work and ministry of the Holy Spirit (Matthew 10:20; Mark 13:11; Luke 11:13; 12:12; John 7:39; 14:16-17; 15:26; 16:7-15).

- Jesus proclaimed that we must be born again by the Holy Spirit (John 3:5-8).

- Jesus offered Himself upon the cross, like a lamb without spot or blemish, through the power of the Holy Spirit (Hebrews 9:14).

- Jesus was resurrected from the dead by the power of the Holy Spirit (Romans 8:11).

- Jesus breathed the Holy Spirit into the disciples after His resurrection (John 20:22).

- Jesus, once exalted to the right hand of God, poured out the Holy Spirit upon the church on the day of Pentecost (Acts 2:1-4, 2:33).

- Jesus instructed the disciples through the ministry of the Holy Spirit (Acts 1:2).

Jesus and the Holy Spirit were always together when He was on this earth. If Jesus needed this kind of ongoing partnership with the Holy Spirit in order to accomplish His divine role in the earth, we must have it too. The Holy Spirit has been sent by Jesus to give you everything you need to be a victorious, successful, faith-filled, overcoming child of God in this world. With Him at your side, you are equipped for every situation in life.

Because no one has ever known the Holy Spirit better than Jesus, we must look to see what Jesus had to say about His personality, His power, His gifts and His character. In John 14, 15 and 16, the Lord Jesus Christ gives us important instruction about how to develop our own partnership with the Holy Spirit.

Jesus Makes Us a Promise

Imagine how difficult it must have been for the disciples to find out that Jesus would be leaving them, especially after walking with Him for three years and seeing Him perform miracle after miracle. Now He was announcing He would soon be returning to heaven.

It was natural for them to feel sorrowful, as if it were the end of their wonderful encounter with the Lord and with the power of God. Living and walking with Jesus was more than they had ever hoped for in this world. With Jesus at their side, their lives had been filled with adventure, excitement, joy, victory, power, healings and miracles.

What would life be like without Jesus? Would it ever be the same? Was this the end to their dream?

Feelings of insecurity and uncertainty would have been normal for any human beings in their shoes. They had grown dependent upon the physical, visible presence of Jesus, something we've never experienced and, therefore, cannot fully comprehend. After He left, they probably felt spiritually abandoned.

In the midst of these fears, Jesus promised them, "I will not leave you comfortless" (John 14:18).

The word *comfortless* is taken from the Greek word *orphanos* (or-fa-nos), which is where we get the word *orphan*.

In New Testament times the word *orphanos* described children left without a father, or it could have described students abandoned by their teacher. In both cases, it is the picture of younger, less educated, less knowledgeable people feeling deserted by those they trusted and looked to for guidance.

Jesus was a spiritual father to the disciples. He knew they were completely reliant upon Him. They could not make it on their own in the world without Him. This is why He promised them, "I will not leave you like orphans."

Two verses earlier He had told them, "And I will pray the Father, and he shall give you another Comforter, that he may abide with you for ever" (John 14:16).

The word *pray* is the Greek word *erotao* (er-o-tah-o), a legal word which is generally used in the Gospels to describe Jesus' prayer life. This particular prayer word indicates that the sending of the Comforter was so crucial to the survival of the disciples that Jesus was going to the Father to present His case for the disciples, almost as if He were legally defending them and their rights.

This case would be so concrete, so clear and so unmistakable that the Father would respond to Jesus' strong request by sending the Comforter, or the Holy Spirit, to the disciples.

It is also important to notice that Jesus said, "And I will pray the Father, and he shall *give....*"

The Holy Spirit was the Father's gift to the church. Peter talked about "the gift of the Holy Spirit" in Acts 2:38 (NKJV). This was the Father's gift, free and without charge to everyone who declared Jesus Christ to be the Lord of their lives. But the Holy Spirit was given in response to Jesus' request for the disciples and for us.

Another Comforter

It was obvious that this Comforter was not a normal person, someone they would be able to see, feel and touch with their hands. Can you imagine the questions that must have been whirling in their minds at that moment?

This is why Jesus was so careful to use key words when He spoke to them about the coming of the Holy Spirit. Especially notice that Jesus used the word *another* in this verse. He says, "And I will pray the Father, and he shall give you *another* Comforter" (italics added).

There are two Greek words for *another*. The first is *allos* (al-los), and the second is *heteros* (het-er-os). *Allos* means "one of the very same kind, same character, same everything, nearly a duplicate." The second word, *heteros,* means "one of another kind or one of a different kind." The word *heteros* is where we get the first part of the word *heterosexual,* which, of course, describes someone who has sexual relations with a person of the opposite sex.

The Greek word used in this text is *allos,* and it conveys a strong message about the Holy Spirit. The verse could be translated, "I will pray the Father, and He will send you someone who is just like Me in every way. He will be identical to Me in the way I speak, the way I think, the way I operate, the way I see things and the way I do things. He will be exactly like Me in every way. If He is here, it will be just as if I am here because we think, behave and operate the same."

Earlier in this chapter Philip had told the Lord, "Shew us the Father, and it sufficeth us" (John 14:8). Jesus had answered him, "Have I been so long time with you, and yet hast thou not known me, Philip? He that hath seen me hath seen the Father; and how sayest thou then, Shew us the Father?" (John 14:9).

Jesus was the exact image of God the Father. Hebrews 1:3 (Amplified) declares, "He is the sole expression of the glory of God [the Light-being, the out-raying or radiance of the divine], and He is the perfect imprint and very image of [God's] nature." Jesus reflected the character of His heavenly Father in every way. If you saw Jesus, then you saw the Father. What Jesus did was exactly what the Father would do.

Jesus gave this testimony about Himself, "Verily, verily, I say unto you, the Son can do nothing of himself, but what he seeth the Father do: for what things soever he doeth, these also doeth the Son likewise. For the Father loveth the Son, and sheweth him all things that himself doeth" (John 5:19-20).

This means Jesus only did what He saw His heavenly Father do. If Jesus healed, it was because it was the Father's will to heal. He never would have acted on His own or out of character with the will of the Father.

If Jesus cast out demons and delivered the demon-oppressed, it was because it was the Father's will to do it. Once again, He never would have acted on His own or done something that was contrary to the will of God.

One of the best ways to discern God's will for certain situations is to look at how Jesus responded to similar situations. People often ask, "How do I know if God wants to heal the sick today?" Look at Jesus for your answer, because He is the perfect imprint of the nature and will of God. Healing power was found by all those who came to Jesus; because Jesus is the perfect imprint of God's nature, this plainly tells us it is God's will to heal.

Your question may be, How do I know whether it is God's will for every person to be delivered from demonic oppression? Once again, look to Jesus for your answer. Every demon-oppressed person who came to Jesus found freedom. This tells us that it is God's will to set every person free who is willing to come to Jesus. The fact that Jesus set them free means He was carrying out the will and the nature of His heavenly Father.

Jesus' life, attitudes and actions were the absolute manifested will of God. By looking at Jesus, you can see the will of the Father. Jesus only did what God the Father would have done. They were in unity in nature, in character, in thought, in deed and in action. That is why Jesus said, "He that hath seen me hath seen the Father" (John 14:9).

When Jesus was teaching the disciples about the Holy Spirit, He took this truth one step further. Just as Jesus is the *exact* image of the Father in every way, now Jesus unmistakably tells the disciples that when the Holy Spirit comes, He will *exactly* represent Jesus in every way. He uses the word *allos* to make this point.

As we have seen, the word *allos* means "one of the very same kind." Jesus had been the "perfect imprint and very image of God's nature." Therefore, the word *allos* tells us the Holy Spirit perfectly represents the life and nature of Jesus Christ. Jesus only did what He saw His heavenly Father doing, and now the Holy Spirit would only do what He saw Jesus doing. As Jesus' representative on earth, He never would act on His own or out of character with the life of Jesus Christ.

I've often heard Christians ask, "I wonder what it must have been like to walk with Jesus. Wouldn't it be wonderful to walk with Him, talk with Him and hear His voice?"

They are missing the point of the Holy Spirit!

The Holy Spirit was sent to bring us the life of Jesus Christ. Just as Jesus told Philip, "If you've seen me, you've seen the Father," now He tells us, "I will pray the Father, and He will give you another Helper who is just like Me in every possible way. If you have Him, it will be just as if you have Me."

We must open our hearts to the Holy Spirit and permit Him to bring us Jesus' life today. He did it for the believers in the book of Acts, and look at the great power they had. Jesus' physical absence did not stop the early church from performing miracles, raising the dead, casting out demons, healing the sick or bringing multitudes to a saving knowledge of Jesus Christ. Because the Holy Spirit was with them, the ministry of Jesus continued to be with them too. The Holy Spirit perfectly represented Jesus to the early church in every way.

Stop looking backward to what you missed by not living two thousand years ago when Jesus walked the earth, and start opening up your heart to the work of the Spirit right now. He wants to represent Jesus to you, your church, your family and your city, just as He did in the book of Acts.

The Holy Spirit and His mission have never changed. We are the ones who have changed. We have limited Him with our unbelief and lack of understanding. Let today be the day you start allowing the Holy Spirit to do what He was sent to do: bring you the life of Jesus Christ in its fullest dimension.

NINE

THE HOLY SPIRIT, OUR COMFORTER

The Holy Spirit was called the Comforter by Jesus (John 14:16). He also used this name in John 14:26, John 15:26 and John 16:7. Calling the Holy Spirit the Comforter must have been very important for Jesus to repeat it four times in the short space of three chapters.

The word *comfort* has many shades of meaning. If you are tired of working long and laborious hours, comfort for you may be rest and relaxation on your couch every evening after work.

If your heart is broken because of a soured relationship,

comfort may mean talking to a friend who will listen to your hurts and allow you to bare your whole soul to them without giving you advice that you already know.

If you feel as if the pressures of life are piling on top of you, and you don't know what to do or where to turn, the comfort you need may be a friend who steps into your situation to help you think through your ordeal, a friend who will assure you that you're still valuable and counsel you about the necessary steps to take next in your life.

If someone you love has just died, it will be comforting for someone to hug and embrace you. It would be nice for them to stay with you through that difficult time of adjustment.

What comfort is to you depends upon where you are and what you are experiencing in life at this moment. This makes it all the more important that we find out exactly what this word *comfort* means. We cannot make a mistake and interpret what Jesus said in light of our own human experience, which varies from person to person.

What does the word *comforter* really mean in John 14:16? The word *comforter* is taken from the Greek word *parakletos* (par-ak-lay-tos). It was first used in a legal sense to denote one who pleaded a case for someone else in a court of law. It described a helper or assistant who was always ready and on standby to help, assist and strengthen.

Parakletos was also used from time to time to denote a personal counselor or adviser. This is the picture of a coach who coaches students and apprentices in the affairs of life, education and business. Just as a coach stands close to his pupils to encourage, exhort, urge, counsel and teach them how to do a better job, a *parakletos* would get very close to those under his or her care.

The Amplified Bible may best translate the word *comforter*. It says, "And I will ask the Father, and He will give you another Comforter (Counselor, Helper, Intercessor, Advocate,

Strengthener and Standby), that He may remain with you forever."

The Holy Spirit Is Alongside of Us

Now that we've looked at the meaning of the Greek word for "comforter," let's look at the parts that make up this word — *para* and *kaleo*.

The word *para* simply means "alongside." It always carries the idea of proximity or geographical location. It specifically speaks of being "very close" or "alongside" to someone or something else. One Greek expositor says it could even be translated "side by side."

Let's look at several examples of the word *para* in the New Testament. The word *para* is used in Luke 5:1: "And it came to pass, that, as the people pressed upon him to hear the word of God, he stood *by* the lake of Gennesaret" (italics added). The word *by* is the word *para*.

This tells us the proximity of where Jesus was standing to preach — *para* or "alongside of" the lake of Gennesaret.

The word *para* is also used in Mark 5:21 in a similar way. After casting a legion of demons out of the demoniac of the Gadarenes, the Bible says, "And when Jesus was passed over again by ship unto the other side, much people gathered unto him: and he was nigh unto the sea."

The phrase "nigh unto" was translated from the word *para*. So many people were pressing forward to touch Jesus that He couldn't even get away from the water's edge. He was forced to walk alongside of the sea. Hence, the word *para* is again used to depict a close proximity to someone or something.

In 2 Timothy 2:2 Paul uses the word *para* to describe his close relationship with Timothy. Paul told Timothy, "And the things that thou hast heard of me among many witnesses, the same commit thou to faithful men, who shall be able to teach others also."

When Paul says, "And the things thou hast learned of me," the word *of* is the Greek word *para*. This is powerful information regarding Paul and Timothy's relationship to one another. Paul was reminding Timothy, "You learned everything *para* me. I allowed you to get alongside of me, and as close to me as you could possibly get. You have learned all of these things by virtue of your close relationship with me."

Paul's use of the word *para* in this verse indicates getting next to someone, as close as you can possibly get, almost becoming one with them. You would never use this word to describe your proximity to a stranger. The word *para* would be used to describe your closest of relationships.

My wife is *para* me. She lives with me, talks with me, shops with me, travels with me, preaches and pastors our church with me, rears our children with me, prays with me. She is always *para* me. We are "side by side, close at hand and alongside of each other" all the time.

When people are close to one another in this way, they affect each other. They may even begin to take on some of that other person's attitudes, feelings, personality traits, habits and gestures. After a while, you know each other so well that you don't even have to ask the other person what they are thinking.

We find a similar experience in a serious discipleship relationship. Paul and Timothy had walked together for many years. To some degree, Timothy probably sounded like Paul when he preached, talked like Paul, picked up some of Paul's gestures and even began to think like Paul. This is normal. Their close relationship allowed the truths of Paul's life to be transferred into Timothy's. After walking with Jesus for three years, the disciples probably started to talk and act like Jesus. That is the purpose of discipleship.

Now that we see what *para* means by itself, let's look at what it means as the first part of the Greek word for

"Comforter" in John 14:16. The first thing this tells us about the Holy Spirit is that He is close by and alongside of us at all times. His relationship with us is not so distant that we must beg and plead for Him to help us. He is always with us in heart, spirit and soul and in physical location.

At the moment of salvation, the Holy Spirit comes to live in us (Ephesians 1:13). While He lives inside us, experientially He is alongside of us to assist us in the affairs of life and to bring the reality of Jesus Christ into our lives. Practically speaking, from that moment on we can draw from His partnership every minute of the day.

The Holy Spirit Has a Specific Mission

The second part of the word *comforter* is the word *kaleo* (ka-le-o), which means "to beckon or to call." For example, Paul used a form of this word in Romans 1:1 when he said he was "called to be an apostle of Jesus Christ."

This is not a picture of someone yelling or calling out for the sake of verbal communication. The *kaleo* kind of calling has purpose and intent, a sense of direction.

For instance, God calls us to fellowship with Him, and He calls unbelievers to repentance and salvation (Matthew 9:13). In addition, both Paul and Peter used the word *kaleo* to describe God's call to salvation and ministry for themselves and others (Romans 1:1; 8:30; 9:11,24; 1 Corinthians 1:9; 7:15; Ephesians 4:1,4; 1 Thessalonians 2:12; Hebrews 9:15; 1 Peter 1:15; 2:9).

Paul specifically used the word *kaleo* to describe his call to apostolic ministry (1 Corinthians 15:9; Galatians 1:15; 2 Timothy 2:9). When he heard the call, it gave him a sense of direction, purpose and destiny. The call of God gave him definition for his life.

Thus, we see that the word *kaleo* carries purpose or destiny or a summoning forth to do something very specific. We are called *to* salvation. We are called *to* the ministry. We are called *to* service in the church and so forth. The call is *to* something.

When someone is called by God to do something, the call gives them insight into the divine purpose, divine intent, divine plan and divine design for their existence. They are summoned forth and specifically called to carry out an assignment at the request of the caller — God.

Because *kaleo* is the second part of the word *comforter,* this means the Holy Spirit has not accidentally assumed His role in our lives. Just as Paul and Peter were called to be apostles, God has called the Holy Spirit to do something very specific in this world. This calling has given the Holy Spirit purpose and direction. You might say it has given Him a job description.

Furthermore, the Holy Spirit must do His job faithfully, knowing that He will answer to the Father, who has given Him this assignment. So what did the Father call the Holy Spirit to do? He is called to be our Helper in the world. This is His chief purpose and responsibility. This is His *calling*.

So when the words *para* and *kaleo* are joined together, they describe someone who is called to help or assist.

Three Features of the Comforter

This chapter has described three important truths that we can glean from the word *comforter* (*parakletos*). We could summarize these truths as follows:

1. The Holy Spirit is close by us.

Doctrinally we understand that the Holy Spirit indwells and seals every believer at the moment of salvation (Ephesians 1:13). But when Jesus referred to the Holy Spirit as the "Comforter" in John 14:16, He was not speaking so much theologically as He was speaking about a practical relationship with the Holy Spirit that we can enjoy on a daily basis.

We do not need to plead and beg for Him to come near

because He is always nearby. As a matter of fact, His place alongside of us is so permanent that Jesus said He would abide with us forever (John 14:16).

Ultimately, by learning to accept and participate in this wonderful fellowship with Him, we will be affected by Him in a powerful way. We will start to take on and produce the fruit of the Holy Spirit in our lives.

2. The Holy Spirit has a calling.

Just as Paul, Peter and other men and women were called into the ministry, the Holy Spirit received a specific "calling" from God the Father to do a specific job in this world.

Just as I am specifically "called" to be a teacher in the body of Christ, the Holy Spirit is specifically "called" (*kaleo*) to be "alongside" (*para*) each believer *at all times*. This means He is with you when you sin, He is with you when you are in the lowest pits of despair, and He is with you when things are going well.

He is with you when you go to bed at night, and He is with you when you get up in the morning. He is with you throughout your day. He is with you when you pray, and He is with you when you don't pray. He is with you when you behave maturely, and He is with you through your moments of immaturity.

He is with you when you go to work, He is with you when you go to the grocery store, He is with you when you go to the beauty salon, He is with you when you go to the ball game, He is with you when you go to the movies, and He is with you when you go to church. Everywhere you go, the Holy Spirit goes too.

If you are a child of God, He is with you at all times, through all circumstances. That is His calling!

3. The Holy Spirit has a job assignment.

The Holy Spirit's job is to help us! That help may include convicting us of sin, empowering us for works of ministry, imparting spiritual gifts, healing other people through us and so on. But these things, as wonderful as they are, are not the total picture. They are simply pieces of a larger picture. The big picture is His helping us. These other things are simply variations of His help.

The Holy Spirit is responsible to carry out His heavenly mission, not according to our demands, human desires, wants and needs, but according to the will of God, the One who called and sent Him to us. This means you and I can be assured that the Holy Spirit will never fail at His job.

TEN

THE
HEAVENLY
COACH

I THINK the best translation of Jesus' prayer in John 14:16 is this: "And I will pray the Father, and he will give you another coach."

Why is the word *coach* my favorite translation of the word *Comforter?* Picture yourself as one of the disciples. You've just seen Jesus ascend back to heaven, and you're standing there, looking up at the sky, thinking about what it had been like to walk with Him on earth for the past three years.

Jesus had been your leader, teacher, mentor, revelator, prophet, miracle worker, healer, pastor and Lord. You had done *nothing* without Him, and He had shown you how to do *everything* you did. He was the center of your life, the focal point of your attention.

Jesus was the One who sent you out to preach and instructed you in what material to preach. He gave you authority to cast out demons, told you how to speak to demons and when not to speak to demons. He taught you how and where to lay hands on the sick.

He showed you how to deal with religious leaders and conduct yourself as a minister of the gospel. He taught you how to hold crusades and build a ministry. He even taught you how to handle money in the ministry (Matthew 10:5-14).

For three years you carefully followed His orders and dared not take a step without consulting Him first. In the truest meaning of the words, Jesus had been your coach. But after His ascension into heaven, He was suddenly gone.

Who would direct you now?

Who would guide you now?

Who would show you how to pray?

Who would show you how to minister?

Who would lead you as Jesus had led you?

Who would coach you in your daily decisions?

We are in the same predicament as the disciples were when Jesus ascended into heaven. We do not have a physical Jesus to turn to and ask questions, to seek for advice or counsel.

Of course, we have the benefit of the Word of God, which reveals Jesus' life, character, thinking, ways and basic truths and commands. However, as to the specific details of life, such as how to pray about a certain situation or what job to take, we cannot arrange a meeting to discuss these issues with Him face-to-face. Through the Holy Spirit, in prayer, we may meet with Him, but physically we cannot. This is one reason we look forward so jubilantly to heaven, when we will finally look on Jesus face-to-face!

Newborns Need Answers

When we come to Christ as newborn babes, direct from a world of sin and spiritual death, we know very little spiritually, if anything at all (1 Peter 2:2). Regardless of how educated we are in natural and intellectual things, we are immature spiritually when we are born again.

Real spiritual maturity takes time to develop in our lives. Some of us were born into the kingdom of God in such ignorance that we didn't even know we had previously been a part of Satan's kingdom.

The early church was comprised of people who had been pagans. They didn't know anything either. Nevertheless, their ignorance did not hinder them from finding their place in Christ and becoming faithful church members God could use. They quickly became a spiritual powerhouse in that dark period of human history.

The good news is that the Holy Spirit has come to teach us everything we need to know — if we'll listen to Him, cooperate with Him and allow Him to do what He was sent to do.

It doesn't really matter what you know or don't know when you received Christ. You have a resident partner in your heart who knows all the answers you need. The quarterback on your team has the winning game plan and the strength and courage you need to achieve victory.

Now you must learn to cooperate with Him. This cooperation is the beginning of the partnership of the Holy Spirit I wrote about earlier. Unfortunately many people have known the Lord for years, which, of course, means the Holy Spirit has indwelt them for years, too. But they didn't know they were supposed to have a communion or partnership with the Holy Spirit so they never developed this dynamic relationship in their lives.

God wants you to know the Holy Spirit in a personal way. He wants you to begin relying upon that relationship the same way Jesus did when He walked the earth. If Jesus needed the Holy Spirit's partnership, then you most certainly need it, too. But how do you develop this relationship? How does a human being relate to the Holy Spirit?

Remember I said the Holy Spirit is like a coach to us? What does a coach do?

If the coach is a baseball coach, he teaches you how to swing that bat and hit the ball. He teaches you how to run from base to base or how to use your glove to catch the ball. Your coach says, "Hold the bat at the base with your hands wrapped around it like this, and when you see that ball coming, swing as hard as you can and hit that ball as far as you can!"

If the coach is an acting coach, then that person teaches you how to become an actor. He will coach you on how to become more convincing, more dramatic and more comical, and even teach you how to cry when tears are necessary for a certain scene.

If the coach is a vocal coach, that person will teach you how to sing, to make your breath last longer, to push from your stomach and make that sound stronger, to sing on key, not flat or sharp, and to sing in a way that really represents the emotional content of the music. A vocal coach will stop you right in the middle of a song to correct you, instruct you and then tell you to go for it again.

A coach teaches, advises, corrects, instructs, trains, tutors, guides, directs and prepares you for your upcoming assignment. If you are new at what you are doing, the *coaching* may include a little *coaxing* as you develop your confidence.

A coach will encourage you as he shows you what you did wrong the last time by telling you how to do it right the next time. "Do it a little different here; press a little harder there; say it a bit louder or softer; move this way; hold the bat that way; don't try so hard here; try harder there" and so on.

A coach isn't there to hit the ball for you, sing that note for you or play the scene for you. He's there to coach *you* so that you can hit the ball, sing the note and perform as you should.

Like an apprentice learning a new job, if you listen carefully, the Holy Spirit will direct and guide you. He'll show you what's needed. He'll open your eyes, impress your mind with supernatural direction, bring you up by the hand, develop, foster, improve and "break you in" on the things of God and life.

This is why 1 John 2:27 says, "But the anointing which ye have received of him abideth in you, and ye need not that any man teach you: but as the same anointing teacheth you of all things."

This verse is not encouraging us to reject the instruction of good leaders but is joyfully telling us that if we do not have a leader, pastor or friend to whom we can turn for instruction, we are not left in ignorance. The Holy Spirit will teach us!

That is why Paul could leave the church in Thessalonica after only having been with them for three weeks of ministry. He knew the Holy Spirit would start teaching them where he left off and that they would continue to grow without him.

We must learn to take the Holy Spirit's advice and follow Him implicitly, taking each of our cues from Him. He must become our heavenly coach, and we must learn to accept His leadership and be willing to yield and concede to His divine guidance with no objections.

The Spirit of Truth

You may be thinking, "But wait a minute! Following the direction of the Holy Spirit is brand new for me. This sounds a little scary to entrust myself completely to the leadership of the Holy Spirit. I can't even see Him, let alone fully surrender myself to His leadership. What is my guarantee that the Holy Spirit will not mislead and misguide me?"

This is why Jesus called the Holy Spirit "the Spirit of truth" three times (John 14:17; 15:26; 16:13). In other words, He was saying, "You can trust the leadership of the Holy Spirit! He has not been sent to lead you down the wrong path, to make a wrong decision or to give you something devilish and evil. He is the Spirit of truth."

You can be sure when He puts a thought in your heart to do something, it is right. When He puts an idea in your mind, it is a right idea. When He nudges your heart to do this or that, it is because He sees and knows something you do not know and, thus, He is trying to guide and direct you. He is always the Spirit of truth, and as the Spirit of truth, you can bank on the fact that He will never mislead you.

Jesus taught for three entire chapters — John 14, 15 and 16 — about the Holy Spirit in order to alleviate the disciples' fears about trusting Him. The bottom line is this: If we are going to move beyond our fear of the unknown and experience real, supernatural Christian living, then we must come to a place of surrender to the Holy Spirit. In this act of surrender, we give permission to Him to be our heavenly coach.

The truth of the matter is, He is always trying to coach and direct us, even when we aren't listening. He is always at our side, speaking, directing, encouraging and trying to help us make the correct decisions and choices in life. Whether we listen to Him or not, He is there because that is the job assignment He has received from God the Father.

Whether or not we benefit from this heavenly coach depends on whether or not we listen to Him and follow His advice.

A baseball coach can't do an athlete any good unless the athlete chooses to follow his instructions. An acting coach can talk until he is blue in the face, and it won't accomplish anything unless the actor is willing to listen and carry out the coach's direction. A vocal coach can see potential in a person's voice and try to coach that singer into singing better. However, if the student refuses to listen and chooses to sing as he or she desires, the coach can't produce the best results.

Likewise, we must give the Holy Spirit ultimate authority in our lives, learn to trust His leadership and do what He instructs us to do. He is a Comforter sent by God to help us. For Him to help us, it requires our ears, our hearts, our trust and our obedience. Anything short of this will produce inferior results, results far short of the supernatural life you really desire. He is there to help you, so let Him help you.

Inadequacy Qualifies You for the Spirit's Help

Let's talk again about telling unbelievers about Jesus. Most believers are terrified to witness. The very thought of sharing Christ with someone makes them tremble. They are afraid they will say something wrong, or they won't know how to answer a question.

The Holy Spirit was sent to witness about Jesus, which means He knows how to do that job (John 15:26; Acts 1:8). If we will allow Him to lead us gently, He will show us how to witness to our friends and neighbors. He knows how to witness.

Praying for the sick is another difficult task for most believers. Many know very little about healing, which often becomes their excuse never to do anything about it. "I can't pray for the sick because I don't know how."

When their pastor exhorts them to get more involved in ministry to the sick, their minds say, "What do you mean, pastor? I thought you were supposed to do that kind of stuff. I didn't know when I came to this church that you were going to ask me to help pray for the sick. I don't know how. I feel totally inadequate."

But the Holy Spirit knows how. He knows exactly why people are sick and why they are not getting healed. He knows if there is bitterness or unforgiveness in their hearts that is hindering them from being healed. He sees it all, and He knows it all. Therefore, He simply needs a willing vessel through whom He may deliver His healing power. The Holy Spirit knows how to heal the sick!

Inadequacy is not an excuse in the kingdom of God. *Inadequacy qualifies you for the help of the Holy Spirit.* The sooner you realize your inadequacies, the sooner you will be released into the supernatural help the Holy Spirit wants to give you.

Being inadequate means the Holy Spirit must become your guide and strengthener. It doesn't matter whether you are trained or not. You have a heavenly coach in your life who knows how to witness and how to heal. If you will listen to Him, read His Word and allow Him to have His rightful place in your life, you will discover Him to be a partner who is right at your side showing you how to witness and how to pray for the sick.

As I have related before in this book, there was a time in my life when I did not know how to witness. I was terrified at the thought of it. "What do you mean, knock on doors? Oh, my, what am I going to say if they answer the door?"

We should train, study and prepare as much as we can to educate ourselves better for witnessing. But it's all in vain unless the Holy Spirit is working alongside of us. Jesus told us, "Ye shall receive power, after that the Holy Ghost is come upon you: and ye shall be witnesses unto me" (Acts 1:8). In John 15:26 Jesus also said, "The Spirit of truth, which proceedeth from the Father, he shall testify of me."

One of the Holy Spirit's favorite things is to talk about and testify of Jesus Christ. Witnessing from the heart comes naturally for the Holy Spirit. If it's so natural and easy for the Holy Spirit, then why does it seem so hard, laborious and joyless when we do it?

The obvious answer is that we're doing it without the partnership of the Holy Spirit. When He is able to work through yielded vessels — believers who have opened their hearts to Him — He pours forth His joy, His excitement, His vitality, His resurrection power upon the lost, and they are saved. Witnessing without acknowledging His help, on the other hand, is a horrible event that I still abhor. If you are really listening to the heavenly coach, witnessing is easy!

But if we aren't yielded to Him so that He can supernaturally testify through us, we often turn to preplanned programs that end up hindering the full release of the Spirit's power and put us in bondage as we witness.

Speaking truthfully from my heart, I believe that if you're not filled with the Holy Spirit and do not intend on learning how to flow in His supernatural life, then you had better stick with those preplanned programs. They will help anyone who is witnessing (even someone who is Spirit-filled). They form a great skeleton, a structure in your mind, to help you get off the ground when you're witnessing.

But without the Holy Spirit's help, you'll be left completely to your own abilities to do the job. You will find that it is very difficult, if not impossible, for your mental abilities and talents to wake up the spiritually dead. No wonder people feel so defeated when they witness without the involvement of the Holy Spirit.

There is a higher and a better way. It is the kind of testifying and witnessing you find in the book of Acts, testifying that shook nations and changed cities. They had no preplanned programs, no witnessing courses, and yet they changed history. Why? They had a relationship with the Holy Spirit, who is the greatest witness and testifier of Jesus in the world! Thus, great success was the result.

The Holy Spirit is still wanting to tell the world about Jesus today. He is still longing to release His power through the church to turn the world upside down with the gospel of Jesus Christ. That's the kind of power the Holy Spirit, our coach, can release through us if we will take our cues from Him and do what He tells us to do.

ELEVEN

BEING
LED BY THE
HOLY SPIRIT

S O OFTEN we just go with the preplanned program and miss what the Holy Spirit is attempting to say and do through us. We have become so programmed in our day that it is amazing He is able to talk to us at all.

There are so many voices speaking to us through books, motivational tapes, church growth seminars and so on that our temptation is to take all of our information and run with it. That information, however, may not contain a single word with which the Holy Spirit wants you to run.

Information is not the same as divine revelation.

As hard as it may seem, most of what we have done has been initiated by us. After the ball is rolling and we've already started "our thing," we pray and ask God to bless what we have initiated — assuming that it is His will because it is a good idea. No wonder we have such poor results.

We must put on the brakes, stop ourselves for awhile and learn to wait until the Holy Spirit speaks clearly to our hearts. Though it may seem as if this way of doing things takes longer, when He does speak, the results will be more rewarding and longer lasting. Furthermore, we can avoid pitfalls which would have cost us a lot of time and effort in the long run.

Learn When to Wait

We must let Him lead us. Take healing, as an example. How many times have you said, "I'm going to go empty all those wheelchairs by praying for those sick people!" After you finished praying and nothing happened, how did you feel? Embarrassed? Defeated? Powerless?

Didn't God want to heal those people? Of course He did, but the anointing may not have been present at that exact moment to heal in that particular way. Being sensitive to the Holy Spirit will help you know when to pray and when to wait.

I think a classic example of this is the account of the two blind beggars in Matthew 9:27-31. These two beggars heard Jesus walking by, but He didn't stop to heal them. The Scripture says that they "followed him, crying and saying, Thou son of David, have mercy on us."

The word *followed* is the Greek word *akoloutheo* (ak-ol-oo-theh-o), which means "to follow after someone or something in a very determined and purposeful manner." Even though they were blind and couldn't see where they were going, they were determined to follow Him until they got His attention.

Look at what they did to get His attention. The verse says they were "crying" out. The word *crying* is the word *krazo* (krad-zo), and it means "to scream, yell, exclaim or to cry out." In other words, they were screaming at the top of their lungs to get Jesus' attention!

This is a very dramatic picture. Think about it. Here are two blind men, desperately wanting to be healed, who are screaming and yelling to get Jesus' attention. But He just continues walking as though they aren't even there. Pursuing Him relentlessly, they grope along in their darkness, still screaming, yelling and crying out for Him to heal them.

He couldn't have missed them because they were yelling so loud. Yet He didn't stop. The whole time they were screaming at the top of their lungs, over and over again, "Have mercy on us! Have mercy on us! Have mercy on us! Jesus, thou son of David...Have mercy on us!"

For years this section of Scripture perplexed me. Why didn't Jesus acknowledge them? Why didn't He heal them? They were so determined to get His attention that they followed Him all the way to the house where He was staying, crying, "Son of David, have mercy on us!"

Finally Jesus asked them, "Do you believe that I can do this?"

They answered, "Yes, Lord."

Then He touched their eyes and said, "According to your faith be it unto you" (v. 29).

Why didn't Jesus stop and heal them when He first saw them? Why didn't He immediately turn to heal them when He knew of their blind condition? And why did He answer them, "According to your faith be it unto you"?

Jesus evidently did not sense the anointing to heal at that moment; otherwise He would have stopped to do it. However, this did not hinder them from receiving. It was as though Jesus said, "I don't sense the anointing to heal right now, so you're going to have to receive this one on your own! Be it unto you according to your own faith."

The only explanation for His not stopping to heal them is that the Holy Spirit was not leading Him to heal at that exact moment. The good news is that they could use their own faith to be healed anyway, and they were healed.

Those whom the Holy Spirit led Jesus to heal, He healed with a perfect, 100-percent success rate. The Bible describes His healing ministry this way: "And the whole multitude sought to touch him: for there went virtue out of him and healed them all" (Luke 6:19).

There are other instances like Luke 5:17, when Jesus was teaching the Word of God and He sensed that "the power of the Lord was present to heal." Following the leading of the Holy Spirit, He ministered to the multitude and healed a paralytic.

Luke 4:1 says Jesus was "led by the Spirit into the wilderness." Luke 4:14 says He "returned from the wilderness in the power of the Spirit." Jesus was Spirit-led in everything He did. He relied totally on the Spirit to guide Him.

Learning to Follow the Leader

We used to play a game called "follow-the-leader" when I was a little boy. I always wanted to be the leader, but my older sister always ended up in that coveted leadership role.

The leader told us what to do, what games we would play or not play, who would clean the house and so on. Basically, we had to do whatever the leader told us to do. No wonder my older sister always wanted to be the leader!

I always think of this when I read Romans 8:14. It says, "For as many as are led by the Spirit of God, they are the sons of God." In Greek the sentence structure is reversed so that it reads, "For as many as by the Spirit are being led, they are the sons of God." It puts the Holy Spirit at the first of the verse, and we are placed behind Him as children who play follow-the-leader.

The Greek word for "led" is the word *ago* (ag-o), which

simply means "to lead." But it must also be pointed out that this word forms the root for the Greek word *agon* (ag-one), which describes an intense conflict, such as a struggle in a wrestling match or a struggle of the human will.

That points out the fact that the Holy Spirit wants to lead us, but our human will does not like the idea of being led. We are often afraid to trust the Holy Spirit. It is the nature of flesh to want to go its own way and distrust another's instruction.

Thus, when we choose to walk in the Spirit and let Him dictate our lives, His leadership over us creates a struggle of our will with our flesh. When I was a child and we played follow-the-leader, I didn't like being led by my sister and being told what to do. I'd rather have been in charge myself and called the shots as I saw them!

However, as children of God, we must learn to stay in our place, which is not in the leader's role but in the follower's role. We are not to be out front directing the Holy Spirit, but we are to go behind Him, following His lead, direction and guidance. The mark of a mature believer is his or her ability to sense where the Lord is leading and then follow that leading.

The fact that the Greek word for "lead" is a part of the Greek word for "struggle" prepares us to deal with our flesh as we proceed into the Spirit-led life. The flesh wants control, so we must mortify (or defeat) the flesh and allow the Holy Spirit to have His way (Romans 8:13; Colossians 3:5). Regardless of how great the struggle seems, this process of mortification and trusting the Holy Spirit's leadership is the only way to live a supernatural Christian life.

In a certain sense, we should make it our goal to be "tagalongs" to see what the Holy Spirit is doing, where He is going and how He is leading, and then follow His leading implicitly. Just as Jesus saw what the Father was doing and did what He saw the Father do, we must be sensitive to see what the Holy Spirit is doing and where He is leading and then follow His cues. That is being "led by the Spirit," which is both the responsibility and the benefit of being a child of God.

To become the mature Christian God wants you to be, you must have this practical relationship with the Holy Spirit.

Giving you an impression or a nudging in your heart to do this or to do that is often the way the Holy Spirit leads. His leading can also be more dramatic, through prophecy or visions or simply a voice speaking to your inner being. Learning to know His voice and to be led by Him should be one of your primary goals as a child of God.

TWELVE

DAILY ADVENTURE WITH THE HOLY SPIRIT

T HE HOLY Spirit sees what we cannot see and knows what we cannot naturally know because He can be everywhere at all times. Human beings, even Jesus in His humanity, are limited in what they can see, hear and know. Therefore, for us to minister successfully, we must listen to the Holy Spirit and allow Him to direct our thoughts, our words and our actions.

Let me give you a simple example of the Holy Spirit's coaching and leading us. One day my wife and I were shopping in a large grocery store. As we walked down the fruit aisle, my wife got a funny look on her face. "Rick," she said, "the Holy Spirit just put it in my heart to go witness to that woman over there. I believe He has given me a specific thing that I am supposed to tell her."

"Then you had better obey the Lord," I told her.

"I'll be back in just a minute," she said.

She went over to the lady and said, "Ma'am, I realize you don't know me, but the Spirit of God told me to come over and tell you something. He said that you think God doesn't love you anymore and that He could never love you again. But He does love you and He wants you to know it."

This woman looked at her as though she were going to slap my wife right on the spot. Her facial expression said, "Get out of my way, you religious fanatic!"

After that reaction, Denise came back feeling like a total failure who had surely mistaken what she was supposed to do. "Rick, maybe I was wrong about the word I gave that woman," she told me. "She sure didn't seem too happy about hearing it."

"Sweetheart, turn around," I said. "That lady is walking toward you right now."

When she turned around, she saw the woman walking toward her with tears streaming down her face. "I just went through a divorce, and someone told me God would never love me again. I don't even know God! Can you pray with me to get saved?"

Right in the fruit aisle of the grocery store, my wife led that dear lady to receive Jesus Christ as her personal Lord and Savior. Her salvation was the product of my wife's partnership with the Holy Spirit. He is the heavenly coach who is called alongside of us to help us in our testimony to the world.

I can see why the Holy Spirit is called the Comforter, because it is so comforting to know that He is alongside of us, especially when He asks us to do something that is different from what we are accustomed to doing.

The Coach's Timing

What a revelation it was when I discovered the gifts of the Holy Spirit were not limited to church services! The gifts of the Spirit can operate anywhere, just as they did in the book of Acts. We can frequently see the gift of miracles, for example, working on the streets of our city. People are healed and set free, just like in Acts 3:1-8, when the crippled man was healed on the steps of the temple.

If we will listen to our heavenly coach, He will nudge us to witness when it's exactly the right moment. He'll put a word in our hearts, a "word of knowledge" (1 Corinthians 12:8), that will supernaturally speak to the heart of someone in need.

One day while I was eating in a restaurant, a waitress walked up to my table to take my order. The Holy Spirit prompted me in my spirit to minister to the waitress. When she left, I asked, "Lord, what do You want me to say to this woman?"

As I sat quietly, thoughts formed in my spirit. I began to understand what He wanted me to say to the waitress. I heard the Holy Spirit — my partner and my heavenly coach — giving me a very specific word of knowledge about this woman's situation in life. It was so specific, I thought, "This is either really right or really wrong!"

I heard the Spirit tell me, "This woman is a single mother who just moved here three weeks ago. She has three children, and she doesn't know how her bills are going to be paid. She is very worried, and I want you to tell her that I am with her in life, especially right now, and that everything is going to work out all right for her. She needs My peace to be ministered to her troubled mind, so speak to her now."

When she came to pour more coffee in my cup, I said, "Excuse me, may I have a word with you?"

She said, "Yeah, what is it?"

I said, "As you turned away from me a few minutes ago,

God spoke to my heart to tell you something. Three weeks ago you moved to this city with very little money. You have three children, and you don't know how you're going to pay your bills. You're feeling like you're all alone in the world, but, you see, God is working in your life. He knows you so well that He has told me to speak this specifically to you today so you'll be aware of the fact that He's with you. You're not alone!"

Tears began streaming down that waitress's face. Every word had been correct. The Spirit of God had met her need because He had a vessel through whom He could speak. That day the partnership of the Holy Spirit helped a hurting woman experience Jesus Christ.

Cooperate

If we will listen, the Holy Spirit will speak to us in ways that seem less spectacular but are still life-changing. He'll tell you when to be quiet at home and stop nagging your husband. He will tell us to be more encouraging. He will exhort us to love our wives in more expressive ways. He will show us how to be better parents and grandparents. He will show us how to be faithful in paying our bills.

If you're thinking, "I've never experienced anything like this before," your problem may be that you are not listening to Him. He's probably talking to you all the time, trying to nudge you to do some of these things. Perhaps you've been ignorant of who was speaking to you, or you were not listening. He's probably putting thoughts and ideas in your heart and mind constantly, but you're not aware it is the Holy Spirit trying to guide and direct you.

The Holy Spirit will conform you to the image of Jesus Christ as you read His Word and seek to develop His divine partnership in your life. He already indwells you. Now you must learn how to enjoy Him and cooperate with Him in your practical, everyday life. He wants to use you to minister to others and to speak to you about your life.

A coach is no good unless you listen to him!

Human beings are generally afraid of the unknown. As we said before, it was for this cause Jesus told us three times that the Comforter was the "Spirit of truth" (John 14:17; 15:26; 16:13).

The Lord knew we could be frightened about following someone we cannot see. After all, if we make a fool of ourselves, we can't say, "It's His fault," and point to someone standing next to us whom everyone can see. And there is also the fear that we are going to go off the deep end and become wild, insane, religious fanatics who live in imaginary worlds.

But the Holy Spirit is "the Spirit of truth," not the spirit of error or deception. He is not going to mislead you, misguide you or hurt you. Nor will He lead you into something that is wrong and destructive to your testimony as a sound Christian thinker and believer. You can maintain a sound mind and be supernaturally led at the same time.

If the Holy Spirit drops a thought into your mind to do something, there is a reason He wants you to do it. If He tells you something will work, it will work. If He gives you instruction, it is because He is trying to help you. He was not sent to you to hurt you or to make a fool of you. He was sent to make you better and more productive, a powerful, stable witness for Jesus Christ.

If your heart is saying, "I really want to know the Holy Spirit this way and I truly do desire to conquer my fears and inward struggles and let Him become My leader," then why not pray:

"Holy Spirit, I want to learn to trust You more. I want to discern Your leadership in my life and allow You to lead, guide and direct me. This is new for me, so please keep speaking, instructing, prompting and nudging me until I break free from my fears and learn to trust You."

THE
RESPONSIBILITY
OF THE HOLY SPIRIT

...and the *responsibility* of the Spirit be with you all.

2 Corinthians 13:14,
author's paraphrase

THIRTEEN

COMFORT
AND
INDWELL

PAUL PRAYED for us to know the "communion of the Holy Spirit." As we have already observed, the word *communion* conveys the ideas of intimacy, partnership and responsibility.

In this section we are going to consider the third point, the responsibility of the Holy Spirit. In John 14, 15 and 16, Jesus spoke about the things the Holy Spirit would do for us, and He specifically mentioned ten things or responsibilities.

The Holy Spirit does many other things. He regenerates us

at salvation, seals us when we are saved, produces the fruit of the Spirit in us, imparts the gifts of the Spirit to us, sanctifies us and so on. All of these are central to His work in our lives.

But the ten aspects of the responsibility of the Holy Spirit which we will emphasize in this next section are those things that He does for us on a *personal* level. They can be summarized as follows:

1. The Holy Spirit comforts us (John 14:16).

2. The Holy Spirit indwells us (John 14:17).

3. The Holy Spirit teaches us (John 14:26).

4. The Holy Spirit reminds us (John 14:26).

5. The Holy Spirit testifies with us (John 15:26).

6. The Holy Spirit convicts us (John 16:9).

7. The Holy Spirit convinces us (John 16:9).

8. The Holy Spirit guides us (John 16:13).

9. The Holy Spirit reveals things to us (John 16:13).

10. The Holy Spirit worships with us (John 16:14).

The first two responsibilities the Holy Spirit does in our hearts. We will begin by reviewing what Jesus taught about the Holy Spirit as Comforter.

1. The Holy Spirit Comforts Us

And I will pray the Father, and he shall give you another Comforter, that he may abide with you forever (John 14:16).

Jesus used the name "Comforter" to describe the Holy Spirit more than any other name (four times). When a truth is repeated over and over again in Scripture, it is repeated for the sake of emphasis.

The word *comforter* comes from the word *parakletos*, which describes a cherished friend who comes to "help, assist, exhort, encourage, counsel, advise and strengthen." It also portrays the idea of a friend who steps into a difficult situation to defend you from something bad or hurtful.

Jesus taught so extensively about the Holy Spirit because He wanted to alleviate any fears or misgivings the disciples may have had about the Holy Spirit, whom they could not see. Above all else, Jesus wanted them to know they could trust the Holy Spirit.

In the years to come, the disciples discovered that Jesus' words had been completely accurate. The Holy Spirit became their closest, most cherished friend and personal adviser.

The Holy Spirit is also our Comforter today. Everything He did for Jesus, everything He did for the disciples and the early church, He still desires to do today. In two thousand years His name, His character, His behavior, His work and His ministry have not changed.

As you go through the circumstances of life, the Holy Spirit is right alongside (*para*) to help you, assist you, defend you, teach you, advise you and strengthen you with every step you take. (I highly recommend that you reread chapter 9 to make sure you understand the work of the Holy Spirit as our Comforter.)

2. The Holy Spirit Indwells Us

Even the Spirit of truth; whom the world cannot receive, because it seeth him not, neither knoweth him: but ye know him; for he dwelleth with you, and shall be in you (John 14:17).

In John 20:22 Jesus breathed on the disciples and told them, "Receive the Holy Spirit" (NKJV). The word *receive* is from the Greek word *lambano* (lam-ban-o), which means "to receive something right now." Because the word *lambano* is used here, it tells us something very important.

Contrary to what some teach, Jesus was not prophesying about the day of Pentecost, when the Spirit "came upon" the disciples. The word *lambano* means that Jesus was imparting the gift of the Holy Spirit to the disciples at that exact moment.

The Old Testament was coming to a grinding halt, and the New Testament was being initiated as the Spirit of God came to live inside the hearts of men for the first time in human history. Up until this time, only Jesus had known the permanent indwelling of the Holy Spirit.

In the past the Holy Spirit had temporarily come upon people to empower them for ministry and service, but He had never permanently lived inside a human being. Even the prophets, priests and kings of the Old Testament never knew this glorious privilege. They only knew the presence of the Holy Spirit in a temporary way. On occasion, He came upon them to do something special but then lifted from them until the next time they needed to be specially empowered for service.

Therefore, when Jesus said the Holy Spirit would *dwell* within the disciples (John 14:17), He was making the most radical kind of statement any Jew could ever speak. He was declaring that, for the first time in history, the Spirit of God was going to be present in the hearts of believers on a long-term basis.

In Greek the word *dwell* is the word *meno* (men-o). It means "to stay or to abide." This is the picture of a person who has resolved that they are never going to move again. They have found the home of their dreams and are determined to stay there. They will not move, budge, flinch or ever be forced to move out.

Jesus uses the word *meno* in John 15:7 when He says, "If ye abide in me, and my words abide in you, ye shall ask what ye will, and it shall be done unto you." The word *abide* is this same Greek word *meno*.

By using the word *meno,* Jesus was saying, "If you have decided to abide in Me permanently, never moving, never wavering, but always constantly abiding in Me, and if My words permanently abide in you, also never moving, never wavering, but constantly having their dwelling place in you, you shall ask what you will, and it shall be done unto you."

This sheds important light on John 15:7. People have prayed this verse with no results and wondered why. The word *meno* gives us the answer to why most prayers are not answered. Jesus is warning us that this promise, "Ask what ye will, and it shall be done unto you," can only be claimed by the most serious Christian.

This is a believer who has chosen to make his heart the permanent dwelling place for the Word of God. He or she has determined to eat, drink, sleep, walk, talk and live constantly in God's Word.

In the same way that God's Word must permanently abide in our hearts, never wavering, never moving, but constantly abiding there, Jesus told us that the Holy Spirit's coming would mark a new time period for mankind when the Spirit would come to dwell in the hearts of all believers permanently.

Dwelling in men's hearts would not be temporary or fleeting as His presence had been in the Old Testament. This was to be a new covenant, based on better promises. He would never move, never waver and never pack His bags to be transferred to another location.

Your heart was not meant to be a hotel. God never intended for the Holy Spirit to be your guest. If the Holy Spirit were only a temporary guest, you could not develop a partnership with Him. But because He has come to stay as a permanent resident in your heart, this is a relationship well worth your time and energy. This partner is with you for the rest of your life, which is another wonderful reason you should begin to develop your partnership with Him right now.

FOURTEEN

TEACH, REMIND AND TESTIFY

THE NEXT three responsibilities that we'll look at are things the Holy Spirit does to help us mature spiritually and minister more effectively to others.

3. The Holy Spirit Teaches Us

But the Comforter, which is the Holy Ghost, whom the Father will send in my name, he shall teach you all things (John 14:26).

Jesus often provides us with human teachers who are very helpful. But, in addition, He gives us a teacher who will never fail us or lead us astray — the Holy Spirit.

Jesus revealed the gospel to Paul through the Holy Spirit. Paul wrote, "But I certify you, brethren, that the gospel which was preached of me is not after man. For I neither received it of man, neither was I taught it, but by the revelation of Jesus Christ" (Galatians 1:11-12).

You will recognize the Holy Spirit's voice by what He says. Jesus said, "He shall not speak of himself; but whatsoever he shall hear, that shall he speak...He shall take of mine, and shall show it unto you" (John 16:13,15).

The Holy Spirit's role as a teacher is to speak for Jesus Christ and not to speak on His own behalf. As Jesus did nothing unless He saw the Father doing it, likewise, the Holy Spirit does nothing unless He sees Jesus directing Him to do so. He carries out the Lordship of Jesus Christ through the church.

Even the gifts of the Holy Spirit declare the testimony of Jesus Christ. That is why Paul told the Corinthians, "That in every thing ye are enriched by him, in all utterance, and in all knowledge; even as the testimony of Christ was confirmed in you" (1 Corinthians 1:5-6).

The Corinthian church was greatly endowed with spiritual gifts (1 Corinthians 1:7). Paul says they were "enriched" by them. The word *enriched* is the Greek word *ploutizo* (plou-tid-zo), which means "to make extremely rich." In today's vernacular we would call this "filthy, stinking rich."

Paul said the Corinthians were particularly rich in utterance and knowledge gifts and stated that the abundance of these gifts confirmed the testimony of Christ among them. Before we go any further, let's look at the words *confirmed* and *testimony*.

The word *confirmed* is the Greek word *bebaioo* (beb-ah-yo-o), which means "to make firm, concrete, stable or solid."

The word *testimony* is *marturion* (mar-too-ree-on), the Greek word that describes a witness or a personal testimony so strong and valid that it could stand up to scrutiny in a court of law and pass the test with flying colors.

The Corinthian church personally knew Jesus Christ as a miracle worker and healer because they had seen the Holy Spirit minister His miracle power in their midst. This confirmed Christ's miracle-working and healing power, making it concrete in their hearts and minds.

Jesus' testimony as a prophet was not difficult for them to grasp either because they had experienced the gift of prophecy so regularly in their midst.

The gifts of the Holy Spirit confirmed the person and work of Jesus Christ. Those gifts gave testimony to the fact that He was still alive, still healing, still working miracles today. By these marvelous gifts, the Holy Spirit teaches us and speaks on behalf of Jesus Christ.

The Holy Spirit also brings us the mind of Christ and the will of God. In regard to this, Paul said, "Eye hath not seen, nor ear heard, neither have entered into the heart of man, the things which God hath prepared for them that love him. But God hath revealed them unto us by his Spirit: for the Spirit searches all things, yea, the deep things of God" (1 Corinthians 2:9-10).

Paul begins this verse by talking about man's inability to understand the deep things of God by himself. It could have been translated, "The heart of man could never dream, imagine or conjure up the things that God hath prepared for them that love Him."

If the human heart could not dream up, even in its wildest imagination, how wonderful the things are which God has prepared for us, then how do we come to know and experience these things? He answers us by saying, "But God hath revealed them unto us by his Spirit."

The word *revealed* is the word *apokalupto* (ap-ok-al-oop-to), which means "to unveil, to reveal or to uncover." It is actually a picture of something that is veiled or hidden when suddenly its veil or covering is removed. As a result, what was hidden for so long now comes into plain view. And God does all of this "by his Spirit."

The Holy Spirit lifts the cover and removes the veil that blocks our view of God's promises to us. By opening the eyes of our spirits to previously veiled truths, He continues teaching us the Word of God, which ultimately testifies to the Lordship of Jesus Christ in our lives.

Furthermore, the Holy Spirit is the one who inspired the Bible. Second Timothy 3:16 says, "All scripture is given by inspiration of God." The Greek word for "inspiration" is *theopneustos* (theh-op-nyoo-stos), which literally means "God-breathed, God-inspired or breathed into by God." The Holy Spirit was the divine agent who did this inspiring of the Bible.

The work of the Holy Spirit to inspire and direct the writing of Scripture does not pertain only to the New Testament. Second Peter 1:21 reveals that the Holy Spirit anointed and inspired the Old Testament writers as well: "For the prophecy came not in old time by the will of man: but holy men of God spake as they were moved by the Holy Ghost."

As the inspirer and author of Old and New Testament Scripture, the Holy Spirit also becomes the ultimate teacher. No one knows the Bible better. No one can teach it better than the One who inspired it and imparted it to the minds of men. That's the Holy Spirit — our great teacher!

4. The Holy Spirit Reminds Us

He shall teach you all things, and bring all things to your remembrance, whatsoever I have said unto you (John 14:26).

Have you ever wondered, "How did the disciples remember everything Jesus taught them?"

Think about it! With all the thousands, even millions of words the disciples heard Jesus speak, how did they ever remember them all correctly? This would require great intellect and a remarkable memory or someone who recorded everything Jesus said when He was on this earth.

This leads us to the fourth responsibility God gave to the Holy Spirit — to bring to our remembrance all the things Jesus did, said and taught.

The Bible gives an example of the reminding work of the Holy Spirit at Jesus' triumphal entry into Jerusalem when the people were joyfully proclaiming, "Hosanna: Blessed is the King of Israel that cometh in the name of the Lord" (John 12:13).

At the time this was happening, the disciples did not realize Old Testament Scripture was being fulfilled before their eyes. John 12:16 goes on to say, "These things understood not his disciples at the first: but when Jesus was glorified, then remembered they that things were written of him, and that they had done these things unto him."

So when John later sat down to write this Gospel, he had the insight to say, "And Jesus, when he had found a young ass, sat thereon; as it is written, Fear not, daughter of Sion: behold, thy King cometh, sitting on an ass's colt" (John 12:14-15, quoting Zechariah 9:9).

After the Holy Spirit was poured out upon them at Pentecost, one of the ways He taught the apostles about Jesus was by tying Old Testament Scripture into events they had experienced with Jesus. Many things which had not been clear or had not made sense to them while Jesus was on earth were now being explained and defined as the Holy Spirit led them to Old Testament verses.

As He inspired the apostles to write the New Testament, He clarified and revealed to them the significance of the Old Testament.

Today all Scripture is written and, according to Revelation 22:18-19, there is nothing we can add to it. There will be no new revelations about the life of Christ. Everything the Holy Spirit wants us to know about it, He has already told us.

One of the most remarkable things about the early church was their fantastic ability to remember what Jesus said and did. Yet some modern scholars try to discredit the Gospels by declaring that they are merely a product of the imperfect memories of the disciples. They argue that the Gospels do not contain the actual words of Jesus. But they have forgotten that part of the work of the Holy Spirit was, and still is, to remind Jesus' followers of everything Jesus said and did.

Therefore, the Gospels contain no errors. What we have in them is exactly what Jesus said and did. They were written as the Holy Spirit put the Gospel writers in remembrance. How marvelous and fantastic it truly is to see how the Holy Spirit illuminated their minds to recall vivid details from Jesus' life and ministry. It is due to this wonderful work of the Holy Spirit that we have the books of Matthew, Mark, Luke and John in our Bibles today.

We can never claim ignorance as our excuse for doing wrong, forgetting what we should do or not knowing Scripture, because the Holy Spirit's purpose is to give us exactly what we need when we need it, helping us think and do what is right at all times. If our partnership with the Holy Spirit is strong, we can lean upon Him the moment our memory fails us because it is His responsibility to remind us of the Word of God.

When we are in the midst of a situation and do not know what to do, the Holy Spirit will reach into the Word of God, withdraw the exact verse or truth we need and put us in remembrance of it at just the right moment.

Perhaps this responsibility of the Holy Spirit is best illustrated in parts of the world where the Bible is illegal. Communist governments have strictly forbidden the printing and distribution of the Word of God for years, yet underground believers in those nations know the Scripture well. In many nations of the world, the Bible is still illegal, but you can also be sure the believers in those nations know the Word of God.

Right now I am living in the former Soviet Union, where the Bible was forbidden for more than seventy years. I am in awe as I meet leaders and entire churches who have had only one Bible through the years. Sometimes it was a hand-copied version with torn and tattered pages from decades of use.

Those yellowed, tattered pages of the Word of God meant everything to them. What respect they have for the Word of God! Not having it has made them love it even more. Those who actually own Bibles hold them close to their hearts and would never lay one on the ground or even leave it sitting on a chair unguarded.

It is the most amazing thing to see people who've had limited access to the Bible and yet know it so well. They can quote it and remember it better than people in free countries who have several Bibles in their houses and the opportunity to read them every morning and every night. Shame on us who have been blessed to have multiple Bibles in our homes yet don't know the Word of God!

There is only one explanation: the Holy Spirit. He is doing exactly what Jesus said He would do: putting them in re-membrance of the Word of God. That is one of His responsi-bilities as our partner in this world.

5. The Holy Spirit Testifies With Us

But when the Comforter is come, whom I will send to you from the Father, even the Spirit of truth, which proceedeth from the Father, he shall testify of me (John 15:26).

As I said in chapter 5, I used to hate witnessing. The word

hate is not too strong a word, because that is precisely what I felt. I hated it.

I loved Jesus with all of my heart, but getting in the car to go knock on doors to talk to people I'd never met in my life and read them a ten-page tract they weren't interested in hearing wasn't my idea of having a good time. Other Christians must have had the same problem because our pastor constantly had to beg and coax our congregation to come to Sunday school visitation and evangelism.

Nevertheless, I knew I was supposed to witness for Jesus Christ. The trouble was that being a witness wasn't what I *was*. It was a job I *did*. I can remember piling into my Sunday school teacher's car, looking at the list of names we were to visit and going to knock on all those doors. I felt so powerless, defeated and joyless as we went. Though many believers would never want to admit it, they feel this way about witnessing too.

The truth is, there is no witness and no testimony without the work of the Holy Spirit. We must have the Holy Spirit's help as we testify. That is why Jesus gave us the fifth point about the Holy Spirit's responsibility to us: "He shall testify of me."

Whether the Spirit's testimony gives you a new revelation of Jesus Christ or directs you to people who are lost, the Holy Spirit loves to testify of Jesus. As a result of His deep love, adoration and affection for Jesus, He loves to talk on and on about Him.

When Jesus told the disciples to stay in Jerusalem to wait for the power of the Holy Spirit, He said, "But ye shall receive power, after that the Holy Ghost is come upon you: and ye shall be witnesses unto me both in Jerusalem, and in all of Judea, and in Samaria, and unto the uttermost part of the earth" (Acts 1:8).

Jesus said the disciples would be witnesses "after" the Holy Spirit came upon them. To witness and testify powerfully about the resurrected Christ, supernatural power is required. Hence, without the Holy Spirit's assistance, it is almost impossible to testify with confidence about Jesus Christ.

Before the day of Pentecost, the disciples were similar to many Christians today. Rather than forcefully advancing upon the world, they were hiding behind closed doors. Unlike the great spiritual army they were supposed to be, they were simply maintaining and "holding out" in the upper room.

Jesus said the Holy Spirit came to testify, but not until Acts 2 did the disciples comprehend the greatness of the Spirit's ability to do that. The witness of Jesus Christ literally blasted out of their mouths as they hit the streets of Jerusalem, fully yielded to the person of the Holy Spirit.

In addition to supernaturally declaring "the wonderful works of God" in other languages (Acts 2:11), they proclaimed the Word of God intelligently in their own language to a people of whom they had been scared to death the day before.

After he received the infilling of the Holy Spirit, Peter boldly proclaimed, "Ye men of Israel, hear these words; Jesus of Nazareth, a man approved by God among you by miracles and wonders and signs, which God did by him in the midst of you...ye have taken, and by wicked hands have crucified...whom God hath raised up, having loosed the pains of death...therefore being by the right hand of God exalted" (Acts 2:22-23,33).

This was supernatural evangelism! This was a supernatural proclamation!

As I said earlier in this book, there is nothing wrong with preplanned evangelism, door-to-door visitation or evangelism programs that teach you the basics of witnessing. But when those programs replace the presence and power of the Holy Spirit, they negate what God meant witnessing to be. Therefore, witnessing becomes a dry, dead, ungratifying, religious work.

Real witnessing or testifying of Jesus Christ can only be

done in relation to the power of the resurrection. This is what Acts 4:33 refers to when it says, "And with great power gave the apostles witness of the resurrection of the Lord Jesus: and great grace was upon them all."

Why lean on your own understanding when it comes to witnessing? Why reduce the power of the resurrection to a mere program? The Holy Spirit was sent to testify of Jesus. No one knows how to testify better than He does.

If you are afraid to witness, as I was, open your heart to the partnership of the Holy Spirit and let Him take responsibility to testify about Jesus through you. As you surrender your heart and mind to the Spirit's control, witnessing will turn from stressful drudgery to a joyful, rewarding and exciting adventure!

FIFTEEN

CONVICT
AND
CONVINCE

THE HOLY Spirit has a complementary ministry to our consciences. He both *convicts* us of sin and *convinces* us of our righteousness.

6. The Holy Spirit Convicts Us

And when he is come, he will reprove the world...of sin, because they believe not on me (John 16:8-9).

Remember when you were a child and you did something

wrong, but you thought no one was watching what you were doing? Then you got caught. Do you remember how it felt, realizing someone had been watching you all along? What horror and dread to be caught in the middle of the act!

You could not lie your way out of such a situation, especially when someone was watching you the whole time. You were unmistakably guilty and could not escape facing your sin. Can you remember feeling so exposed?

This is what a sinner feels the first time the Holy Spirit convicts him of sin. It is amazing how long a sinner can live without conviction, without sorrow for his behavior, nearly numb to the feelings of the wrongness about his actions.

The Bible says sin has made them to be hard-hearted, spiritually blind and past feeling (Ephesians 4:18-19). Compound this with the fact that they are spiritually dead and therefore unable to respond to God, and you find out why lost people can do what they do over and over again.

But those factors change instantaneously when the Holy Spirit touches the human soul and exposes its sinful condition. Exposed, naked, embarrassed — confronted — is exactly what a sinner feels when the Holy Spirit wakes him up to his real spiritual condition.

Jesus said the Holy Spirit would *reprove* the world of sin. The word *reprove* is the Greek word *elegcho* (el-eng-kho). It means "to expose, to convict or to cross-examine for the purpose of conviction," as in convicting a lawbreaker in a court of law.

By the time the Holy Spirit is finished dealing with the lost, sinful soul, that lost person will feel exposed and convicted. As the Holy Spirit enables him to hear the Word of God for the first time, that Word is so razor sharp that it penetrates his soul until he feels as if he has been cross-examined on a witness stand. Finally, the court is adjourned, the verdict is announced, and he is declared guilty.

That is the work of the Holy Spirit to convict sinners of their lost condition. The whole world stands guilty before

God (Romans 3:19), but the whole world doesn't realize it is guilty.

Jesus taught that "no man can come unto me, except the Father...draw him" (John 6:44). No one argues that this drawing is done through the work of the Holy Spirit. Jesus reminded us of this when He said, "And when he is come, he will reprove the world of sin" (John 16:8).

Without the work of the Holy Spirit to expose our sinful condition, we would still be in darkness today, eternally lost and without God.

It is frustrating to share Christ with family and friends and to feel as if you are "hitting a brick wall." You share, talk and plead with them to receive Christ, yet it seems they just can't hear what you are saying. Even though they know they are sinners, they don't seem to be convicted by this knowledge. Ignoring that horrible fact, they press on as though they were numb or ignorant of the degree of spiritual decay in their lives.

The Bible says the lost person is "dead in trespasses and sins" (Ephesians 2:1). Dead people don't feel anything. They especially don't feel the conviction of sin. It requires a special, supernatural work of the Holy Spirit to rouse the human consciousness to its sinful condition.

How can you make a dead man see? He is dead. How can you cause a dead man to feel? It is impossible for a dead man to respond. How can you convince a dead man that he needs to change?

Thanks to the Holy Spirit's call that touched our souls, we were awakened to our sinfulness, and the Spirit beckoned us to Christ. Once we were brought to this horrible place of undeniable conviction, recognizing we were sinners, the Spirit invited us to come to God. At that divine moment, our souls heard Him say, "Awake thou that sleepest, and arise from the dead, and Christ shall give thee light" (Ephesians 5:14).

What a miracle that God raised our spirits from spiritual

death to spiritual life. There is no greater miracle! This convicting work of the Holy Spirit is the first thing the Holy Spirit ever does in our lives, and it is not the last.

7. The Holy Spirit Convinces Us

And when he is come, he will reprove...of righteousness, because I go to my Father, and ye see me no more (John 15:10).

Have you ever complimented someone who argued with you, rejecting your compliment and essentially questioning your judgment in the matter? For example, rather than thanking you after you said the person looked as if he had lost weight, he responds by telling you how fat he is.

"Well, I've gained a lot of weight, and I look so fat now. I wish you could have seen me three months ago when I really looked good! I don't look as good now." This is the equivalent of throwing the compliment back in your face. It would be far more polite to be gracious and say, "Thank you. I'm so glad you noticed. I appreciate your telling me I look better."

Here is another example. Someone sings a solo during a church service that deeply stirs your heart. At the end of the service, you make your way through the congregation to find the soloist. He or she responds to your compliment, "Thanks for the compliment, but I thought I did a horrible job tonight. I can't believe I sang so badly. I don't know how you got anything out of it."

It's rude to do this. It is rejecting the love, admiration and appreciation God is expressing through someone else to encourage you. It's the same as saying, "I appreciate your giving me this compliment, but we both know it isn't true, so you don't have to say it." In effect, that person is calling you a liar!

People who do this don't intend to be ill-mannered. When someone compliments you, don't try to convince the person

121

of how bad you are or how terribly you performed. Learn to accept the compliment.

We do this to God every day! This is why Jesus told us about a very special responsibility the Holy Spirit has concerning our lives: The Holy Spirit comes to convince us of righteousness.

Second Corinthians 5:21 declares, "For he hath made him to be sin for us, who knew no sin; that we might be made the righteousness of God in him." What a wonderful work God did for us!

He sent Jesus to die in our place and to take our sin upon Himself. He exerted all of His mighty power to raise Him from the dead, seated Him at His own right hand and then sent the Holy Spirit to live in us so we could become "the righteousness of God in him."

Yet, if there is any subject in Scripture about which Christians will argue, it is this question of righteousness. Most Christians are so conscious of their old sinful nature, which still abides in their flesh, that they can't embrace the truth that they have been declared righteous. Tell them they are good, and they respond by telling you how bad they are.

Sinful nature always clings to what is the worst and most negative. It will always gravitate downward, never upward. That is the nature of the mind that is not under the temperance and control of the Holy Spirit.

This is why lost people can do such inhumane things. The sinful flesh, if not mortified by the sanctifying power of the Holy Spirit, will ultimately follow its negative leanings all the way to the grave.

If abandoned to your flesh, you'll never believe a good report, you'll never believe God is doing a good work in you, and you'll certainly never believe you have been made "the righteousness of God in him."

Negative, base, sinful thinking has been a part of our humanity for so long that it requires a special convincing work of the Holy Spirit to make us realize what God has done in us.

If the Holy Spirit doesn't do this special work to convince us of our right standing with God, when God says, "You're My child. I have made you righteous. You are beautiful to Me," our negatively charged mind and emotions will retort, "It's not so! I'm unworthy. I'm unholy. I'm so pitiful!"

Again, this is like throwing the compliment back in God's face! Imagine it: He put forth His best work to redeem us and make us "new creations," and we have nothing good to say about ourselves (2 Corinthians 5:17).

The Bible tells us we are "his workmanship, created in Christ Jesus" (Ephesians 2:10). Another translation of that verse could be, "We are a product of His very own, marvelously created in Christ Jesus — that is, created under the influence and control of His divine power."

This is powerful, life-changing truth, but it takes the Holy Spirit to move this truth from our heads to our hearts.

Just as the Holy Spirit must *convict* the sinner of his lost condition, He also must *convince* believers of their new right standing with God.

We are so negative in our old, fleshly nature that it takes a supernatural work of God to make us comprehend our new condition in Christ Jesus. This realization is just as supernatural as the lost man recognizing He is lost. Only this time we are being awakened to the fact that we are righteous!

I can remember when the Holy Spirit woke me up to this truth many years ago. Driving down the street, feeling totally unrighteous, I was listening to a teaching tape on righteousness. Suddenly my mind began to grasp what I was hearing. It was as if someone took blinders off my eyes and earplugs out of my ears. For the first time I was seeing and hearing the truth about my new righteousness in Christ Jesus.

This truth was going straight to my heart by the power of the Holy Spirit! I heard it. I understood it. My inward man leaped for joy when the Spirit of God illumined my understanding about righteousness. He convinced me of the truth, and I was set free!

If you struggle with your self-image and feelings of condemnation, you need the Holy Spirit to do His convincing work in your life. Only He can open your eyes to see who you have become eternally in Christ Jesus.

Once your eyes have been opened and you understand you are righteous, you will never again throw the truth back in God's face and argue with Him. Now when the Holy Spirit reminds you that you have been declared righteous, you will cry out with joy, "Thank You! That's exactly what I am!"

You don't have to keep being negative about yourself all the time. You don't have to beat yourself over the head, constantly reminding yourself of how unworthy you are. Jesus Christ made you worthy. He made you righteous! He made you a new creation.

Why is this so important?

Because if you don't have a grasp of this God-given righteousness, which is the only basis for a good self-image, you will never know who you really are and what your purpose in life is. Furthermore, a negative self-image will inhibit your ability to pray with confidence and trust God to answer and to live a life free of guilt and condemnation.

A false understanding of righteousness is that it comes only after you go to heaven but has no part of your life on earth. This misunderstanding causes a cloud of guilt and condemnation to hang over you for the rest of your life, hindering your ability to walk in the joy and victory of the Lord.

The convincing work of the Holy Spirit is not an option for those who want to progress as mature Christians. The Holy Spirit takes this responsibility seriously. It is a necessity.

SIXTEEN

GUIDE, REVEAL AND WORSHIP

THE LAST three responsibilities of the Holy Spirit that Jesus taught about in John 14, 15 and 16 concern the Spirit's work through our actions.

8. The Holy Spirit Guides Us

Have you ever asked, "What am I supposed to do with my life? What direction am I supposed to take? How can I know for certain I am doing what God really wants me to do?"

These are hard questions, and we have all asked them

over and over again. While the Bible contains God's revelation of Himself to man, it does not always answer our specific questions about the details of daily life — for example, what job we should take or what person we should marry.

The Bible gives us guiding principles for our choices in life, such as to abstain from the appearance of evil (1 Thessalonians 5:22) or not to be yoked with unbelievers (2 Corinthians 6:14). From these principles we can make the decisions not to take a job as a bartender or marry a person who has not committed his or her life to Jesus Christ.

We must commit ourselves to study and memorize the Word of God, hiding it in our hearts so we will not sin against God (Psalm 119:11). Then, knowing and being guided by God's Word, we should make fewer mistakes in our choices as we move along in life.

Nevertheless, as wonderful as these principles are, they don't tell us specifically which job to take or what person to marry! Sometimes we need guidance, direction and answers that are not written in the Scriptures, and Jesus said the Holy Spirit would give us this kind of guidance. "He will guide you into all the truth" (John 16:13).

Divine guidance in our daily lives is one of the biggest challenges we face in the Christian life. Thus we have another tremendous responsibility of the Holy Spirit — telling us what to do and when to do it every step of the way.

This guiding work of the Holy Spirit was crucial to the early church. They trusted the leadership of the Holy Spirit to guide them in the formation of doctrine, the selection of leaders, where to minister, whom to send on certain missionary journeys and so forth.

It's interesting to note that before the Holy Spirit was poured out upon them in Acts 2, the disciples tried to make a big decision without His help. They decided to choose a replacement for Judas, who had killed himself after he betrayed Jesus. They had narrowed it down to two men,

"Joseph called Barsabas, who was surnamed Justus, and Mat-thias" (Acts 1:23).

Remember that Jesus, just before He ascended, had in-structed them to go directly to Jerusalem and tarry until the Holy Ghost came upon them (Luke 24:49). In essence He was saying, "Go to Jerusalem, and don't do one single, soli-tary thing or make any decisions whatsoever until you are endowed with power from the Holy Spirit!"

They went to Jerusalem and waited. But then they seemed to get a little impatient and started to look for something to do. Peter got the bright idea that someone ought to replace Judas. After they came up with two candidates, this was what happened:

> And they prayed, and said, Thou, Lord, which knowest the hearts of all men, show whether of these two thou hast chosen, that he may take part of this ministry and apostleship, from which Judas by transgression fell, that he might go to his own place. And they gave forth their lots; and the lot fell upon Matthias; and he was numbered with the eleven apostles (Acts 1:24-26).

Without the Holy Spirit there was no communication with Jesus, so the Bible says they "cast lots" to decide between the two men. In other words, they made the decision by a roll of the dice! This episode is even more interesting when you consider that the Bible never mentions Matthias again.

Contrast this event with those that occurred after the Holy Spirit was given on the day of Pentecost, and you find an incredibly awesome difference. For one thing, never again did the apostles use a roll of the dice to make a decision.

Let's look at a few of these examples from the book of Acts. You will see that, in addition to guiding us into the truth of the Bible, the Holy Spirit also has a guiding hand in the daily affairs of our lives if we will allow Him to do so.

In Acts 13:2 we read, "As they ministered to the Lord, and fasted, the Holy Ghost said, Separate me Barnabas and Saul for the work whereunto I have called them." This marked the point where the apostle Paul was sent out on his first missionary journey. He was to accompany Barnabas, who had been spending the last few years discipling him.

In Acts 15 the apostles and elders in Jerusalem sent Paul and Barnabas to Antioch with a letter containing the following message: "For it seemed good to the Holy Ghost, and to us, to lay upon you no greater burden than these necessary things" (Acts 15:28).

At that time there was a great doctrinal dispute going on in the church regarding how much of the Old Testament law should be kept by gentile believers — for example, circumcision, the Sabbath and so forth. In this letter the elders gave the saints at Antioch the conclusions which they and the Holy Spirit had reached and agreed upon together.

Just a short time later Paul was planning to go into several different places to preach the gospel, but the Holy Spirit told him not to go. "Now when they had gone throughout Phrygia and the region of Galatia, and were forbidden of the Holy Ghost to preach the word in Asia, after they were come to Mysia, they assayed to go into Bithynia: but the Spirit suffered them not" (Acts 16:6-7).

All of these accounts in the book of Acts say one very important thing to us: We cannot know what to do, where to go, whom to go with and when to go there without the guidance and direction of the Holy Spirit.

We also see that He can lead us in two ways — by yes or by no! He will try to stop us from doing something that looks good to us but is either a trap of the enemy or not God's will, or He will open a door of opportunity and give us total peace to walk through it.

What a relief and security it gives us to know that God the Father has given the Holy Spirit the responsibility of leading us, guiding us and even warning us away from certain people, places and situations. This is His job. And if we will listen to Him, we will fulfill our calling and purpose in this life.

9. The Holy Spirit Reveals to Us

> For he shall not speak of himself; but whatsoever he shall hear, that shall he speak: and he will shew you things to come (John 16:13).

We have already discussed how one of the Holy Spirit's responsibilities is to represent Jesus to us and to be our communication link with Him. Jesus said that the Holy Spirit would not say or do anything He did not hear or see from Jesus, just as Jesus did not say or do anything He did not hear or see from the Father.

Whatever the Holy Spirit reveals to us, we can be sure that it is coming straight from the throne room of God. We can trust what He is saying to us, whether it has to do with how we are living our lives, what our calling and purpose are, which job to take, whom to marry or how to deal with our children.

The Holy Spirit will most often reveal things to us during times of prayer. One of the most widely quoted Scripture verses for the Holy Spirit's involvement in prayer, and one of my personal favorites, is Romans 8:26: "Likewise the Spirit also helpeth our infirmities: for we know not what we should pray for as we ought."

This verse is packed with nuggets from the Greek which will sharpen our understanding about the Holy Spirit's active role in revealing what we need to know in our daily lives.

Have you ever experienced a time when you did not know what to pray for yourself or someone else? Have you ever been in a terrible dilemma, and you did not know how to get out of it?

Maybe you have said, "Lord, the desire of my heart is so

deep, but my mind is so confused. I'm not even sure if I know what the desire of my heart really is! Lord, please help me to pray." That's when we thank God for Romans 8:26. This verse shows the Holy Spirit's responsibility to reveal to us the will or wisdom of God for our lives through prayer.

The most important thing to realize is that prayer is not something we do by ourselves. Prayer is a two-way conversation between us and the Holy Ghost, an outgrowth and manifestation of the intimacy and partnership we share with Him. During this intimate time of communication, He reveals where Jesus is going with a certain situation and what He wants us to do or not do.

The very first part of Romans 8:26 says, "Likewise the Spirit also helpeth." What does that mean? The Greek word for "helpeth" is a compound word. The first part of the word means "to do something in conjunction with somebody else." The second part means "to receive." Together they say "to take hold of something with somebody else."

"Helpeth" conveys the idea of real partnership and cooperation between two individuals who are working together toward the same end. It is not one person doing one part of the job and another person doing another part but two intimate friends and partners giving all they have to solve a problem, overcome an obstacle, defeat an enemy, handle a difficult situation or understand a dilemma.

Together, you and the Holy Spirit will reach that supernatural peace that passes all understanding because He will reveal to you how to think, what to say and what to do about a matter.

Let's continue with Romans 8:26: "Likewise the Spirit also helpeth our infirmities." The word *infirmities* is the Greek word *astheneia* (as-then-i-ah), which really should be translated "weaknesses." This word describes people who are weak, sick or broken down in their bodies, minds or emotions. Frequently, it is used to describe those who have lost their spiritual well-being and strength and may not even know why.

The Holy Spirit will reveal your infirmities and help you with them. Some things are obvious, but even obvious problems may have something hidden which only the Holy Spirit knows. Therefore, we depend upon His leading and direction in all things, just as Jesus did during His ministry on earth.

He may be warning you of an attack of the enemy or a hindrance to finances or telling you why you haven't been healed of an illness so that you can be healed. Or He might show you that you have been overtaken by a fault — an addiction or an obsession He is urging you to eliminate from your life. He knows these are weights that are holding you back from fulfilling your destiny.

Whatever the Holy Spirit is revealing to you, you can be sure He will live up to His responsibility. He will come right alongside you and reveal to you everything you need to know to turn your problem into a victory.

"Likewise the Spirit also helpeth our infirmities: for we know not what we should pray for as we ought." In the literal Greek, that last part simply means "we do not have the know-how when it comes to prayer."

The most skilled and experienced intercessors are the ones who, no matter what the situation, will turn immediately to their most intimate friend and partner, the Holy Spirit, and make certain they are on the right track in prayer.

All of us are occasionally confronted with a crisis or a decision about which we don't know how to pray. This is part of our human, limited condition, and it is this "infirmity" the Holy Ghost comes to remove. He comes to give us the know-how. He makes up for whatever we lack.

"For we know not what we should pray for as we ought." The word *what* is an interesting word in the Greek. It means "the very exact little thing." We don't know the fine points, the details or the real root of the problem with which we are dealing. We simply are not able to see all of the facts and have a comprehensive view.

We need divine guidance and help to locate and handle all the fine little details and fiery darts with which the enemy is bombarding us. We need the mind of Christ to deal with these, and we have the mind of Christ when we are putting the full weight of responsibility upon our partner, obeying His instructions, saying what He says and doing what He does.

As a flawed human being with many quirks and blind spots, I am so grateful God has given the Holy Spirit this responsibility over me. Whenever I am in the dark about anything, my first and foremost prayer partner will reveal to me whatever I need to know for whatever I am going through.

10. The Holy Spirit Worships With Us

He shall glorify me (John 16:14).

In this verse of Scripture, Jesus is telling us that one of the responsibilities of the Holy Spirit is to glorify Him. Now the Holy Spirit is an invisible, nonmaterial spirit being, and as such He cannot glorify Jesus without using someone or something to do so. I'm sure you have guessed by now that the vessel He chooses to use to glorify Jesus is the one in which He lives — *you!*

Just how does the Holy Spirit fulfill His responsibility to glorify Jesus Christ through you? First, He can heal the sick, cast out demons and lead lost people to the saving knowledge of Jesus Christ through you. These acts certainly glorify Jesus in a magnificent way.

But when we are talking about the communion of the Holy Spirit, we come to another more intimate and equally important way in which the Holy Spirit glorifies Jesus through you — in acts of praise and worship.

I spoke earlier of the first charismatic meeting I attended, which was held in a charismatic believer's home. With all the strange things that happened that evening, the one thing that captivated me and ultimately drove me to continue with the charismatic movement was the praise and worship.

During that time of praise and worship among those who were filled with the Holy Spirit, I experienced the presence of my Savior and Lord Jesus Christ more than I ever had before. It was as though He were standing right in front of me, so close that I could feel His breath on my face and sense the warmth of His body.

In this intimate, personal time of lifting our hands and hearts to God, I became "drunk" with the presence of Jesus, just as Paul exhorts us to be in Ephesians 5:18-19: "And be not drunk with wine, wherein is excess; but be filled with the Spirit; speaking to yourselves in psalms and hymns and spiritual songs, singing and making melody in your heart to the Lord."

As I left that meeting, even while I was sorting through my thoughts, I found myself thinking about praising and worshipping the Lord and making melody in my heart to Him. I was like a child who had just tasted ice cream for the first time — I wanted more and more and more. I wanted every aspect of Jesus to come pouring through me in a brand-new, powerful and personal way.

As I look back upon that experience now, I can see that because I was filled with the Holy Spirit, all I could think about and long for was more of Jesus. That is because all the Holy Spirit thinks about and longs for is Jesus. All He wants to do is magnify, lift up, exalt and glorify Jesus,

This is a responsibility of the Holy Spirit that is always grand and glorious and totally pleasurable to believers who allow Him to move this way in their lives. Nothing else fulfills and satisfies the spirit and heart and soul of man so much.

Worshipping the Lord in communion with the Holy Spirit is what makes Jesus Christ real in our daily lives.

THE PERSONALITY
OF THE
HOLY SPIRIT

"And grieve not the holy Spirit of God, whereby
ye are sealed unto the day of redemption."

Ephesians 4:30

SEVENTEEN

THE JEALOUSY
OF THE
HOLY SPIRIT

YE ADULTERERS and adulteresses, know ye not that friendship of the world is enmity with God? Whosoever therefore will be a friend of the world is the enemy of God. Do ye think that the scripture saith in vain, The spirit that dwelleth in us lusteth to envy?" (James 4:4-5).

Since we are studying how to develop a more intimate and personal relationship with the Holy Spirit, these verses are particularly important for us.

James accuses his readers of committing adultery. This is

especially strong when you consider that he was writing to good, stable, moral Jewish believers. Even before they became Christians, they would never have dreamed of committing sexual adultery. Adulterers and adulteresses were stoned to death.

James couldn't have said anything more shocking, hurtful or outrageous. Imagine if a great spiritual leader wrote to you and called you an adulterer or adulteress. For a Jew, nothing was more insulting than this.

This leads me to ask the question, If they were good, moral people who would never commit sexual adultery, why did James call them adulterers and adulteresses?

James continued by asking, "Know ye not that the friendship of the world is enmity with God?"

These believers were having too close of a relationship with the world. To drive this point into their hearts, James called them adulterers and adulteresses.

The King James Version mentions both "adulterers and adulteresses." But the Greek version of the New Testament simply says "ye adulteresses." Later I will tell you why this is important.

The word *adultery* has all kinds of connotations. Unfaithfulness, impurity and violating a commitment to marriage are just a few. We normally associate adultery with a spouse who has a sexual relationship outside of his or her marriage.

When this is found out, the violated spouse feels so deeply hurt that nothing else in the world can be compared to it. The death of a spouse would not be as difficult to deal with as a spouse who has committed adultery.

Feelings of rejection, betrayal, being lied to, misled and deceived are some of the terribly strong and painful emotions the spouse feels when the sanctity and security of the marriage relationship has been recklessly thrown away by the adulterer or adulteress.

Many years ago my wife and I were the ministers for the

single adults in a large Southern Baptist church. We developed a program to help those who were newly divorced. We found that most of these people felt they were outcasts from the church. When we opened our hearts to minister to them and made "life after divorce" a well-known emphasis of our ministry, newly divorced people came to us from all over that region.

In one year's time we ministered to about eight hundred people who had just been through a divorce. It was one of the most gratifying, yet troublesome, periods of ministry we have ever experienced. It was gratifying to see people who had been so rejected and wounded being healed by the love of Jesus Christ, but it was troublesome to hear what many of these precious people felt as a result of being betrayed by someone they trusted.

Day after day we would sit and listen as each one told us his or her story. Out of a hundred cases, seventy sounded identical — so identical that eventually I could finish most of their stories.

Again and again these precious and broken people said, "I just don't know how he could do that to me! After all these years of being faithful to him...after raising our children together...after working to help him through school...How could he do this to me?...I gave my life to him the best I knew how. How could he dump me and go after someone else?"

Or, "How could she do this to me after I've given her so much...I gave her my love, my attention, all that I knew to do...How could she do this to me?"

In nearly every session we would hear something similar to "I feel as if my heart has been ripped out and stomped on!" Betrayal by a spouse is possibly the worst betrayal of all. Nothing hurts worse, cuts deeper or lasts longer than this type of emotional trauma.

Remember that I said I would explain why the Greek just says "adulteresses" instead of "*adulterers* and adulteresses."

James wrote his book for the members of the church, which is the bride of Christ. In some way that James does not describe, they had gone outside their relationship with Christ to find fulfillment and companionship with someone or something else. Therefore, they were unfaithful to their spouse, Jesus Christ, and became adulteresses.

When believers do this, the Holy Spirit feels the hurt and grief of a violated spouse. When we really understand that sin not only affects us, but also the indwelling Holy Spirit, it changes our permissive attitude toward sin and causes us to live more holy lives for Him.

James called these good, moral Jewish believers "adulteresses" because they went outside of their marriage to Christ to find fulfillment. They were giving their lives, minds and hearts to worldly things.

They had committed *spiritual adultery*.

The Error of Comparing Ourselves to Others

Compared to the world, these believers looked holy and religious. They were moral, honest and hardworking people. If they looked at themselves and then at the world around them, they probably scored fairly high in their own eyes.

But there is no comparison between us and the world. They are lost; we are saved. They are in sin; we are called to be holy. They are carnal; we are to be spiritual. They smell of death, while we are the fragrance of life. Therefore, we can never measure our fruitfulness, our holiness or our success against the lost world that surrounds us. This would be like comparing apples to oranges. They simply can't compare.

It is also a mistake to judge yourself by what you see in other believers' lives. You are who you are, and they are who they are. You cannot judge your relationship with Christ by the relationship you think others have with Him.

They have not stood where you have stood, and you have not walked in their shoes either. They may be more mature than you, or you may be more mature than they. Therefore, how can you compare yourself to them? Looking at others is no way to make a judgment on how well you are doing.

Churches and ministries often make the same mistake. Rather than judge themselves according to the specific mandate God gave them and how well they are doing in fulfilling it, they look to see how other churches or ministries are doing. If they look bigger and better in comparison to the rest, they often mistakenly assume they are doing "pretty good" and may even feel gratified about their work.

The church of Ephesus was the biggest church in New Testament times. It was the epitome of what a church should be. Everyone wanted to visit and preach in the church of Ephesus. This church prided itself on sound doctrine and sound thinking and on its hardworking believers.

Had we been able to look at the church of Ephesus, we probably would have agreed it was the model church, a "perfect" example of what every church should be. Here is the church where we'd all be happy to claim our membership.

Yet when Jesus spoke to the church of Ephesus in the book of Revelation, He said, "Nevertheless I have somewhat against thee, because thou hast left thy first love. Remember therefore from whence thou art fallen" (Revelation 2:4-5).

In the Greek language the word *fallen* speaks of an already completed condition. In other words, they weren't in the *process* of falling. They had *already* fallen!

While the Christian community and church leaders praised them, Jesus said they were completely fallen and backslidden. They looked sparkling compared to the rest of the church world, but in Jesus' eyes they had fallen short of the mark He had set for them. Only He knew that mark; hence, only He could know how far short they had fallen.

God knows it all. He foreknew us, He predestined us, and He called us to be conformed to the image of His Son. We should never be satisfied with where we are in our spiritual growth until we reach that ultimate goal of being conformed to the image of Jesus Christ.

What Has God Told You?

I know what God has called me to do. I have heard Him say things to me I have never told anyone else. These words were meant only for my spiritual ears to hear. Though I know what He called me to do, and I know what I am currently doing, I have not yet reached the goal that has been set before me.

Others who have never taken a step of faith may see my walk of faith as an example to be imitated. They may see me to be something special, or perhaps someone may see you in this same way. But they did not hear the mandate God gave me and therefore cannot know whether or not I have fallen short. Compared to where they are, I may look advanced, but compared to where I am supposed to be, I may have fallen short.

This must be what Paul felt when he said, "Not as though I had already attained, either were already perfect: but I follow after, if that I may apprehend that for which also I am apprehended of Christ Jesus. Brethren, I count not myself to have apprehended: but this one thing I do, forgetting those things which are behind, and reaching forth unto those things which are before, I press toward the mark for the prize of the high calling of God in Christ Jesus" (Philippians 3:12-14).

Paul received more revelation than anyone else we know. He moved in incredible power, raised up church leaders, wrote the bulk of the New Testament and withstood terrible bouts of persecution. We talk about him; we read his epistles; we use him as an example to be followed. Yet when he wrote this verse, he knew he had yet to attain all he was called to attain.

In the midst of all his successes, Paul chose to look into the future. He refused to be stopped by gloating over his own accomplishments and instead decided to keep striving for "the mark for the prize of the high calling of God in Christ Jesus."

Paul also refused to be affected by the approval or disapproval of other people. That is why he said, "But with me it is a very small thing that I should be judged of you, or of man's judgment: yea, I judge not mine own self. For I know nothing by myself; yet am I not hereby justified: but he that judgeth me is the Lord" (1 Corinthians 4:3-4).

Paul was saying, "Your opinion or my opinion of me is not what's important. What the Lord thinks is important. He is the One who judges me!"

The point I am making is this: We are poor judges of ourselves. We either think too much of ourselves or too little of ourselves. The last thing we need to do is compare ourselves to others and then deem our progress by what we see in them. Other people are not the issue in your life. *You* are the issue!

Are you doing what God told *you* to do? Are you being all God called you to be? Are you faithfully fulfilling the mandate God gave you to fulfill? Are you living the holy life God called you to live? Are you praying as God called you to pray? Are you giving as God told you to give? Are you teaching the Bible and praying with your children as God told you to do? Are you breaking the habits the Holy Spirit has convicted you to break?

Stop comparing yourself to others. When you stand before the judgment seat of Christ, He is not going to say, "In comparison to everyone else, you did well." At that moment, which we will all face someday, only you will be the issue.

His eyes of fire will be set on *you* at that moment, and no one else will matter.

As His blazing eyes penetrate your spirit and soul, the question will be: "Did you do what I called you to do? Were you everything I asked you to be? Did you try to be all you could be for Me?"

We will stand utterly naked and exposed before Him, with no one to blame and no one with whom to compare ourselves. It will be between us and Him. That is why Paul said, "The Lord...will bring to light the hidden things of darkness, and will make manifest the counsels of the hearts: and then shall every man have praise of God" (1 Corinthians 4:5).

James was writing to people who were good in comparison to the rest of the world. But in the eyes of Jesus they had committed a gross sin. They had entered into an unhealthy "friendship with the world" that violated their relationship with the Lord.

What Is Friendship With the World?

The word *friendship* is from the word *phileo* (fil-eh-o). It is one of several Greek words for "love" used in the New Testament. Just for a moment, let's look at these various words for "love" so we can better understand the difference between them and *phileo*.

The word *agape* (ag-ah-pay) describes divine love. This is the word used in John 3:16 when the Bible says, "For God so loved the world, that he gave his only begotten Son." This divine love stands in its own category. It is a love that gives without any condition and without any thought of return. This is the kind of love the New Testament commands us to develop for one another in our lives. It is the highest and best kind of love.

The second Greek word for "love" is *eros* (er-ahs), which denotes a sexual relationship between a man and a

142

woman. It is where we get the word *erotic*. This word is not found in the New Testament, and I believe there is a good reason.

The sexual relationship between a Christian husband and wife should aspire to a higher kind of love. *Eros* is natural and to be expected between a husband and wife, but *eros* needs to be coupled with *agape* to create a relationship that is not self-serving or self-seeking.

The husband and wife who put a foundation of *agape* under *eros* will emphasize giving to each other more than receiving from each other. This will put *eros* in the place God designed for it to be in our lives.

The third word for "love" is the word *phileo*. It describes a friendly kind of love. It is the most commonly used word for "love" in the Greek language of the New Testament period. Because it was so widely used at that time, no one could have mistaken what James was saying when he used the word *phileo*.

Phileo carries the idea of an intense fondness that is developed between people who enjoy each other's company. It describes love between family members. It speaks of two or more people who know one another, who are fond of one another and who are growing more deeply involved in each other's lives. The word *phileo* describes a relationship that is built by choice and not by necessity.

Though the word *phileo* had no religious meaning in the Greek world, its various forms are used fifty-four times in the New Testament. For example, it is where we get the name for the city of Philadelphia in Revelation 3:7.

Philadelphia is taken from the words *phileo* and *adelphos*. The word *phileo* means "friend," and *adelphos* is the Greek word for "brother." Therefore, the two words together mean "the city of friendly and brotherly love."

Usually the word *phileo* conveys the idea of a friend with whom you desire to have a deeper relationship. In a certain sense, this attraction is so great that it leads to being preoccupied with someone or something. It involves giving your attention, your time, your devotion, your love and so on. That is what friendship demands if it is a friendship to be maintained through the years.

The word *phileo* can describe two young people who have fallen in love with one another. To say they are attracted to one another would be an understatement. They are hopelessly addicted to one another! They are always thinking of what the other person is doing and when they will see each other again. They are consumed and preoccupied with each other. Stop just for a moment and think back to the first time you really fell in love, and you will remember the condition I am describing right now.

That is precisely the condition James was talking about when he said, "The friendship of the world is enmity with God" (James 4:4). He wasn't judging these believers for having expensive tastes, having good jobs, desiring nice houses or driving beautiful cars. The phrase "friendship of the world" was not about owning things but rather about being consumed or preoccupied with the things of this world.

Those to whom James was writing were getting tangled up in the system, the thinking, the behavior and the material possessions of the world. One reason we know they were struggling with this tendency to worldliness is found in the same chapter.

Here James said their prayers weren't being answered because they were asking God for things with wrong motives. Rather than desiring things so they could help others, they selfishly wanted more and more things for themselves. James told them, "Ye ask, and receive not, because ye ask amiss, that ye may consume it upon your lusts" (4:3).

They were Jewish believers who always had lived holy lives, and now they were being seduced by the things of the world. They were seduced to the point of being attracted to, consumed with and preoccupied with the world. This attraction had already become so great that they had entered into friendship with the world. They had gone outside of their relationship with Christ to give their hearts and minds to something else. In a spiritual way they had committed adultery.

James isn't teaching that having nice possessions is wrong. Rather he is telling us it is wrong to be so consumed and preoccupied with the things of the world that you never think of anything else. Flirting with the world will eventually lead to an ungodly connection with the things of the world.

It is spiritual adultery toward the Lord Jesus Christ to be so involved with the current status quo of society that you think as they do, act as they do and seek the same things they do. Having things in your hand is one thing, but having things in your heart is another.

When things of the world get in your heart and you become preoccupied with them, you have crossed a serious line.

Talking Yourself Into Sin

James went on to say, "Whosoever therefore will be a friend of the world...." I especially want you to notice the words "will be" in this phrase. They are taken from the Greek word *boulomai* (boo-lom-ahee), which means "to counsel" or "to resolve."

This word *boulomai* could describe a counseling session, or it could describe seeking the counsel of someone else. As it is used in this verse, the word *boulomai* does not describe some other counselor who listens to you and advises you. This time the counselor is *you*! You are counseling yourself.

This is a snapshot of a Christian who is being seduced by the world. Rather than saying a firm no to ungodliness, as Titus 2:12 instructs, he chooses to draw nearer to the world for a closer look. In essence, it is this "flirting" with sin that eventually leads to the practice of it.

This is a Christian who feels his flesh being lured by the world. Sensing the warning of the Holy Spirit to draw away from the situation and walk in holiness, he turns a deaf ear to the Spirit in order to listen to his flesh. Before he knows it, he is talking himself into doing what he knows is wrong.

He may say, "Well, I know I shouldn't, but just a little won't hurt...." "I know it will probably grieve the Holy Spirit, but God will forgive me...." "I can't believe I'm doing this, and I know I shouldn't, but I'm going to do it just this time...."

This person literally talks (in other words, "counsels") himself into doing what he knows is wrong. This is the process of sin in the soul. It is seducing and deceptive. It tries to lure the soul to lay aside convictions and to follow the dictates of the flesh to carnal, beastly pleasures that last only for a moment.

Now a word of caution: Don't categorize this kind of behavior as only the more gross sins of the flesh. You don't have to commit sexual immorality to be worldly. The Holy Spirit may have been convicting you about being too materialistic. He may be convicting you about gossip, speaking rudely to your spouse, lying and cheating, being unfaithful in your tithes and offerings, or some other thing.

If God has told you to give an offering, and you opt to buy something for yourself instead, you have declared that your priorities are out of line. You probably talked yourself into feeling "all right" about not giving. "Come on — you give all the time...you don't have to obey this time. Anyway, it's probably not the Lord really telling you to give...."

Every time the Spirit of God tells you to give, your flesh will tell you it's not really God. Your flesh is being *attracted* to something else, and unless you decide to crucify the flesh, that *thing* will become more important to you than doing the will of God. If that is you, then worldliness is already wrapping its arms around you.

If the Holy Spirit has convicted you about gossiping, then stop it. If you continue, you are choosing not to surrender your tongue to the Spirit's control. As a result, you have chosen to talk and act like the world.

You've probably heard your flesh talking to you, coaxing you by saying, "You probably shouldn't say this, but go ahead anyway...They won't tell anyone...Besides, maybe you can tell them to pray about it...Yes, you're not supposed to tell anyone this information, but no one else will know you told it...."

If the Holy Spirit has convicted you about the way you speak to your husband or wife, yet you continue to speak abusively and disrespectfully, you are choosing to reject the Spirit's control and go your own way. The world acts like this. By rejecting the Spirit's control, you are choosing to be worldly.

It is amazing how well we can talk (or counsel) ourselves into being ugly to our spouses. "I have a right to feel this way...I'm tired and I don't care what you think right now...Just leave me alone...I have needs too...."

You wouldn't speak that way to anyone you work with during the day, so what gives you the right to speak to your spouse that way when you get home at night? What gives you the right to take your anger out on your husband at night? When you became a Christian, you lost all those rights.

Being a Christian husband or wife necessitates that you crucify the flesh and live in the presence of God. Without the sanctifying power of the Spirit, you can't be a good spouse. Without His help, you'll behave and act as an ungodly person might.

If the Holy Spirit has convicted you about exaggerating the facts when you tell them, then it is wrong for you to keep exaggerating the facts. It ceases to be exaggeration and becomes lying.

When the crowd is listening and laughing at your story, but the Holy Spirit convicts you to stop exaggerating, then it's wrong! But the flesh will argue, "It's not entirely true, but they're all enjoying it...The way you tell it is so funny...Only you know it's not entirely true, so go ahead and enjoy yourself...."

By rejecting the Holy Spirit's correction, you are choosing to be no different from the world. You are opting to be worldly.

Tempted to Tolerate

Worldliness tries to wrap its arms around all of us. Just think of the things you tolerate in your life today, things you would never have tolerated ten years ago. Do you watch movies today that you would have considered a sin ten years ago? Be honest!

Are you more liberal in your thinking about sin now than you used to be? Are there any areas of your life that used to be more on fire and less compromising than they are right now? Do you pray and witness as you once did? You might as well be honest with God because He knows your real spiritual condition anyway.

You can't bluff God by saying, "Well, here is the reason I didn't obey You...I would have done what You said, but...." If you're worldly in some area of your life, just say, "Yes, I'm worldly in this area of my life." At least being honest with God will put you in a place where God can deal with your heart. Guilty means guilty. Once your guilt is realized and admitted, then you're on honest territory with God, and you can grow again.

We could all admit worldliness in some area of our lives, but if we do not deal with these areas as the Holy Spirit leads us, over time we will become more conformed to the world than to Jesus Christ.

Being a friend to the world doesn't happen overnight. It

takes time. Very slowly, seductively and methodically, our thinking, our behavior, our outlook on life grow to look more and more similar to that of the world than to that of Jesus.

This is what James meant when he said, "Whosoever therefore will be...." Those words "will be" are very important for you and me. It means our sin is our responsibility. We cannot blame our behavior on our environment, on our friends or anything else. If we lose what we have in terms of spiritual fire, it is because we have counseled ourselves into believing sin is acceptable when it is not. We are the result of our own resolution.

James was speaking to Christians who had counseled themselves into doing what they would never have dreamed of doing before.

It is as though James says, "If you've become the friend of the world, it's because you've made so many little exceptions for yourself that now the things that used to bother you don't bother you at all. As a matter of fact, over a period of time you've become a worldly Christian with worldly thinking and worldly behavior!"

EIGHTEEN

GRIEVING THE HOLY SPIRIT

A
ND GRIEVE not the holy Spirit of God, whereby ye are sealed unto the day of redemption" (Ephesians 4:30).

This verse tells us how all those little exceptions we make when we "counsel" ourselves into sin affect the Holy Spirit. If we are wanting to develop intimate communion with Him, the last thing we want to do is grieve Him.

The word *grieve* is from the Greek word *lupete* (lu-pe-te). This was a very special word. It was used to denote the emotions of a betrayed spouse, similar to the emotions I described in the previous chapter. Betrayed, deceived, being lied to, misled, hurt, wounded and abused — all of these vividly portray the emotions of a spouse who has discovered his or her mate has been unfaithful.

Now we find the word *lupete* is used by Paul to describe how we affect the indwelling Holy Spirit when we tend to worldliness. There is no doubt as to what Paul is telling us. When we cease to make our relationship with the Holy Spirit the number one priority in our lives and let other things take His rightful place, it hurts Him the same way it hurts a spouse to find that his or her mate has been unfaithful.

Jesus is Lord, but the Holy Spirit is the One who lives in us, leads us, guides us, teaches us, reminds us, comforts us, seals us, sanctifies us, empowers us and works to produce the character of Christ in us. He has been sent to reveal the will of God, which is the mind of Christ, and to give us the victory that Christ won through the cross and the resurrection. He is here for us. That is why He was sent.

Therefore, when we ignore Him, turn a deaf ear to Him or consistently disobey what He nudges us to do, it grieves Him. It would grieve you too if you were the Holy Spirit. Just think of it! But let's be even more specific about what grieves the Holy Spirit.

The verses preceding this one about grieving Him say to put away "lying" (4:25), "let not the sun go down upon your wrath" (4:26), "neither give place to the devil" (4:27), "steal no more" (4:28), "let no corrupt communication proceed out of your mouth" (4:29) and, finally, "let all bitterness, and wrath, and anger, and clamour, and evil speaking, be put away from you, with all malice" (4:31).

These things grieve the Holy Spirit. Unfortunately, Paul was speaking to Christians when he wrote these verses. That means Christians were doing these things. They were lying, holding on to grudges, giving place to the devil, stealing, talking evil about one another, giving bitterness a place in their hearts, being angry and having malice toward each other.

151

No wonder the Holy Spirit was grieved. He had come to produce holiness in them, but worldliness was dominating their lives, and they were quenching Him. He was being left out of the picture.

The fact that Paul used the word *grieve* (*lupete*) tells us the Holy Spirit felt abused and wounded by the wrong behavior and attitudes of the Ephesian church. He felt like a spouse who was being dragged through the mud by an unfaithful mate. After doing all He had done within them, how could they now push Him aside and give in to their flesh in such a manner?

We need to think before we talk and act.

We need to remember that Someone lives inside us whose name is the Holy Spirit. The reason He is called the Holy Spirit is because He is holy. Romans 1:4 calls Him "the spirit of holiness." That is who He is, and that is what He comes to produce in our lives.

You would never think of throwing mud and garbage all over a beautiful cathedral. Your conscience couldn't bear the guilt of knowing you had personally destroyed a finely decorated church building. Yet *you* are even more than that. The Holy Spirit doesn't live in buildings; He lives in *you*.

In spite of this, we throw mud and garbage into our lives all the time, not thinking of how it must grieve the Spirit of holiness who lives inside us. We drag Him through the mud of our lives when we sin deliberately.

According to Ephesians 4, the sins that Christians find hardest to resist aren't usually ones such as drunkenness or sexual impurity. We don't normally commit those outward sins. The sins we must deal with are inward attitudes such as grudges, bitterness, anger or malice. If for no other reason, we should not allow these attitudes because we know they grieve the Holy Spirit.

The next time you want to hold resentment in your heart toward someone, ask yourself the question, Is this attitude going to grieve the Holy Spirit in my life?

If we simply make ourselves more aware of the Spirit's indwelling presence, it will help to change the way we think and live. It will most definitely help us to think before we talk and act. Remember that the Holy Spirit lives inside you. What you do in your life today, you do to Him as well. Where you go today, you take Him with you. When you go to the movies, He goes with you. When you choose to sin, you are dragging Him with you through that filth.

Do you really want to grieve Him? Of course not! Think of it. The Holy Spirit lives in you and deserves your respect.

Can a Christian Be an Enemy of God?

Being a worldly Christian is serious business. That is why James 4:4 says, "A friend of the world is the enemy of God."

Notice the word *is*. It's the Greek word *kathistemi* (kath-is-tay-mee), which means "to constitute" or "to render." Christians who choose to take a worldly path have set themselves in opposition to the godly path God desires for them. As a result of their own choice, they have rendered or constituted themselves to be the enemies of God.

The word *enemy* in James 4:4 is from the Greek word *echthros* (ekh-thros), which describes an extremely opposite attitude to love and friendship. Whereas love and friendship mean warmth, commitment and relationship, the word *echthros* means extreme hostility, intense disrespect and an all-consuming hatred.

Romans 8:31 declares, "If God be for us, who can be against us?" By the same token, if God is against us, then who can be for us? If God is against us, we are finished in our pursuits and nothing but frustration lies in our future.

James is telling us: "If you choose warmth and friendship with the world, this will put you in direct opposition to God." That is not a good place to be.

If you choose friendship with God, on the other hand, this will place you in direct opposition to the friendship of the world. This opposition is so strong that it makes us enemies with the world. Again, the word *enemy* carries the idea of hatred.

Jesus used the word *hate* when He said, "No man can serve two masters: for either he will hate the one, and love the other; or else he will hold to the one, and despise the other. Ye cannot serve God and mammon" (Matthew 6:24).

According to Jesus, it is impossible for a Christian to give his heart simultaneously to two masters. So we must choose whom we are going to serve: God or mammon. *Mammon* was an expression used by the Jewish community of that time to express the idea of worldliness.

The word *serve* comes from the word *doulos* (doo-los). It is where we get the word for a servant or slave. This word was used to denote a servant who had given himself over entirely to another person or thing. This person was a slave for a lifetime.

This slave "serviced" something or someone with all of his attention, time and energy. By serviced, I mean he catered to his master's every wish, desire or demand. He was there to help, assist and fulfill his master's wants and dreams and had no time for any other thing.

When you buy a car, washing machine or even a house, it must be serviced to keep it in working order. These things will operate for a while without your attention, but in time you must give your attention to them in order to keep them in good running condition. If you own a house, you know a house requires all kinds of time, attention, energy and money.

When Jesus said, "Ye cannot serve God and mammon," He was giving us this very important truth. Both God and mammon are going to require time, attention, energy and money. There is not enough of you to service both God and worldliness in your life. Hence, you must choose which you will service.

Serving God means spending time with Him, learning to know His voice, developing a pattern of obedience in your daily walk. It will require you to serve God your entire life. It will demand your fullest attention. The work of God must be serviced with prayer, obedience, repentance and worship.

The good news is that Jesus promised that if we would seek Him first, He would make certain that everything we needed in a material way would be added to us (Matthew 6:33). That is supernatural living.

Serving mammon (the world) means giving your fullest attention to material pursuits. If you're going to be successful according to the world's standards, you won't have room for anything else in your life. Serving mammon will require all your time, attention, energy and money.

That is why Jesus said we must hate one master and love the other. We must hold to one master and despise the other.

Whom Do You Serve?

Let me ask you this question: What are you serving in your life right now? What most requires your time and attention? Can you truthfully say you are giving God your fullest attention, that the chief priority in your life is to serve and obey Him?

Or must you confess that worldly pursuits, possessions and corporate success consume your energies?

If you're consumed with God, these other things have a lower place on your list of priorities. But if you're consumed with the friendship of the world, then material things will dominate the landscape of your mind.

Just stop and ask yourself, "What do I think about more than anything else in life?" Your answer will probably tell you whom you are serving with your time and talents.

God will stand in opposition to the Christian who is outside the life He has planned for him. That is why James 4:6 says, "God resisteth the proud."

The word *resisteth* is the Greek word *antisteste* (an-tee-ste-te) from *anthistemi* (an-tee-stem-mee), and it means "to

155

stand against, to oppose, to take a stand against another." A believer who has chosen to go his own way has chosen to take a stand against God. If this believer does not repent and come back to where God wants him to be, God will oppose him and take a stand against him. That Christian can rebuke the devil's power all day long, but it will be to no avail. His problem is not the devil. His problem is God.

I can't imagine anything worse than a Christian who is being opposed by God. Things just don't seem to work right or turn out the way they should. The path of worldliness is a hard road for a believer to take.

If God is standing against us, our plans will fail, our dreams will come to nought, and nothing in life will succeed. Frustration, worry, anxiety and feelings of failure are just a few of the negative emotions we will feel if God is blocking our way.

This resistance from God, as terrible as it may sound, is an act of God's grace. By blocking our ways and resisting our choices, God's precious Holy Spirit endeavors to bring us to a place of sweet brokenness where sin is confessed and fellowship with Him is restored.

But why is this so serious with God? Why are our choices and our behavior so crucial that it would cause almighty God to respond in such a strong way? If our life is ours, and we can choose what we want, why would God be so offended by the Christian who has chosen to take this other path?

NINETEEN

A
PERMANENT
INDWELLER

D O YOU think that the scripture saith in vain, The spirit that dwelleth in us lusteth to envy?" (James 4:5).

This verse explains why God reacts so strongly to Christians who get wrapped up in worldiness instead of the Holy Spirit.

I'm convinced it is a basic lack of understanding that permits believers to do the wrong things they do. If they understood who lived in them and how holy the Holy Spirit was, they wouldn't want to hurt and grieve Him. We need more teaching on the person and work of the Holy Spirit.

Understanding the internal work of the Spirit in our lives is central to our being saved, being sanctified and being empowered for daily service. How do we think we can proceed in the power of God without this basic foundation in place? This is not optional. This foundational knowledge is a necessity.

In light of this, let's look at what James meant when he wrote, "Do ye think the scripture saith in vain, The spirit that dwelleth in us lusteth to envy?"

There are three key words that we must consider in this verse of Scripture: 1) dwelleth, 2) lusteth and 3) envy.

First of all, we must look at the word *dwelleth*. In chapter 13 of this book, we saw that when the Holy Spirit came to live in us at our new birth, He came to be a permanent indweller.

The word *dwelleth* used in John 14:17, which we discussed earlier, was *meno*, which means "to permanently abide or dwell." But in James 4:5 the word *dwelleth* is taken from the Greek word *katoikizo* (kat-oy-kee-zo).

Katoikizo is a compound of the words *kata* (kat-a) and *oikos* (oy-kos). The word *kata* means "according to," and *oikos* is the Greek word for a "house." Taken together it means "to take up residency" or "to dwell in a house."

This word carries the idea of residing permanently. In other words, this word would never describe a transient or one who only came to live in a place temporarily. This is the picture of a person who was born, reared, married, had children, worked, retired, died and was buried all in the same city. He never wanted to go anywhere else, live anywhere else or move away. This was his home, and he wanted this city to be his home forever.

In other words, when the Holy Spirit came to live in us, it wasn't for a short period of time. When He came, He came to stay. From this point onward, He made your heart His home. He has, so to speak, hung His own pictures on the walls of your heart, laid His own rugs on the floor, moved His furniture in, settled down into a nice, big, comfortable chair and has no intention of ever leaving to live somewhere else.

The Holy Spirit has come to be a permanent indweller in your heart. Your heart is not a hotel to which He comes to visit occasionally. Your heart is His home. He is the One who lives inside you and never leaves.

A Cathedral for the Spirit

In a figure of speech, I have said the Holy Spirit hung pictures on the wall, put rugs on the floor and settled into a comfortable chair. But He has done much more. He has taken our spirits, which were dead in trespasses and sin, raised them to new life and recreated them to be the marvelous temple of God.

Obviously, what the Holy Spirit accomplished in our salvation was not just a decorating job. He created something inside you so wonderful, so marvelous, so fantastic and outstanding that God, the Holy Spirit, was willing to make it His home.

Paul referred to this miraculous work when he wrote, "What? Know ye not that your body is the temple of the Holy Ghost which is in you, which ye have of God, and ye are not your own? For ye are bought with a price: therefore glorify God in your body, and in your spirit, which are God's" (1 Corinthians 6:19-20).

The word *temple* is taken from the word *naos* (nah-os), which always describes a highly decorated shrine. By shrine, I mean something like a beautiful cathedral which has tall, vaulted ceilings, marble columns, granite floors, hand-carved woodwork that is overlaid with gold and silver, crystal chandeliers, silver candelabras and burning incense around the front of the altar.

Being raised a Southern Baptist, I was accustomed to the interior of a Baptist church. We had pews, a baptistry, nice carpet and heavy oak pulpit furniture. That was our style of church decoration. It was nice, but moderate and simple.

The first time I entered a cathedral, I nearly fell over. I was just a small boy when I participated in my uncle's wedding at a large Catholic church in our city. I remember walking down the aisle of that church building awestruck by how high the ceilings were and how beautiful the statues and paintings were.

In my journeys from one end of the former Soviet Union to the other, I often stop to see the large Russian Orthodox church buildings that cover the land. The architecture, the craftsmanship, the gold, the silver, the precious stones, the inlaid marble, the paintings and the icons are more beautiful than I can imagine talent to create them. Some of these buildings are nearly unbelievable in terms of size, beauty and intensity. To say they are spectacular is downplaying their beauty.

This is precisely what Paul meant when he said we were temples of the Holy Spirit. It is warm and cozy to think of the Holy Spirit making Himself at home in our spiritual houses. I personally appreciate meditating on the permanence of the Spirit in our lives in this way.

But because Paul used the word *naos* (temple) in 1 Corinthians 6:19 to describe us, he is painting a very different picture.

The Holy Spirit did the ultimate miracle when He came to dwell in our hearts. He took our spirits, which were dead in trespasses and sin (Ephesians 2:1), and quickened us together with Christ (Ephesians 2:5). In that miraculous moment He created us to be like God in righteousness and true holiness (Ephesians 4:24).

This work inside us was so glorious and perfect that when it was all finished He declared we were His workmanship, created in Christ Jesus (Ephesians 2:10). From start to finish we were apprehended by Him, regenerated by Him, and molded and fashioned by Him to be the temple of the Spirit of God.

This makes salvation the greatest miracle of all.

The change in our previously dead spiritual nature is truly

miraculous. He resurrected it and filled it with glory, power, revelation, holiness, splendor, righteousness, the fruit of the Spirit, the gifts of the Spirit, and the life and character of Christ. He adorned our inner man until, spiritually speaking, we became a shrine.

Inwardly we are so beautiful and magnificently created that almighty God, through His Spirit, is willing to take up permanent residency within us. What kind of home do you think God would require? A shabby shack made of dirt and sticks? No! He has built for Himself a beautiful temple within our hearts.

What You See Is Not What You Get!

Most of us have poor self-images. We see ourselves as unworthy shacks built of mud and sticks. We certainly do not see ourselves as highly decorated shrines of the Holy Spirit. And, naturally speaking, we are fairly weak as human beings.

Paul was aware of this too, and that is why he commented, "But we have this treasure in earthen vessels, that the excellency of the power may be of God, and not of us" (2 Corinthians 4:7).

Paul uses several key words in this text. First of all he says, "But we have...." The Greek word used here is *echomen* (ekh-o-men), and it can be translated "we hold" or "we possess." It is in agreement with the phrase "earthen vessels," which is the Greek word *ostrakinos* (os-tra-kin-os), describing small, cheap, easily broken pottery. This particular kind of pottery was considered to be weak, fragile and valueless.

By using the word *echomen* in connection with the *ostrakinos,* Paul is making a strong statement regarding our real spiritual condition. He says that we hold, contain or possess some kind of treasure in vessels that are small, cheap, easily broken and basically valueless. That is how he describes our physical bodies.

He's right. The human body is fragile. A wrong diet can kill it; working too hard can break it; too much pressure can damage it; and even after caring tenderly for it your whole lifetime, it still dies.

The greatest minds, the most creative inventors, the highest intellects, the most colorful writers and the most talented politicians all die. Eventually the human body breaks under the stress of age, and the vessel which carried such incredible talent and potential is reduced to unrecognizable dust, totally valueless. Some human vessels break earlier, and some last longer, but eventually they all break, they all collapse, and they all return to dust.

Here is the amazing part: We earthen vessels contain or hold something Paul called a treasure. The word *treasure* is the word *thesauros* (the-sau-ros). It describes a treasure so rich and so immense that it could never be expended. This would be the treasure hunter's greatest dream. This time we have the treasure map. As always, *X* marks the spot for hidden treasure, and this time the Bible has written the *X* on us. We are the hiding place for secret treasure.

From natural appearances, we may look weak, fragile and valueless. Certainly we do not look like a place where God would hide His greatest treasure. Paul wrote this Scripture verse with a sense of amazement: "We hold this immense, incredibly rich, inexhaustible treasure in these human bodies of ours that are so easily broken and expended!"

If you were God and had a treasure so grand, would you place it in something as unreliable as you are? But that is what He did. This is part of the miracle of salvation.

What we see with our eyes is weak humanity, but contained in that fleshly, carnal, short-lived body is the very power that created the universe and raised Jesus from the dead.

The point is this: After recreating us in Christ Jesus, after turning our previously dead spirits into temples so marvelous that God is willing to live in them, and after placing His greatest treasure in our hearts, do you think the Holy Spirit is going to walk off and leave His investment?

He has put all of His energies and riches into you to make you a dwelling place worthy for God. He called you, sealed you, sanctified you and filled you with His holiness. Inside — in your human spirit — you are the highly decorated shrine of God.

That is why Paul went on to admonish the Corinthians by saying, "For ye are bought with a price: therefore glorify God in your body...and spirit" (1 Corinthians 6:20).

In the oldest Greek versions of 1 Corinthians 6:20, Paul only admonished them to glorify God in the body rather than in the body *and the spirit.*

That's because your body is the issue in this verse, not your spirit. Your spirit is inhabited by the Holy Spirit. Our problem is not our human spirits, where the Holy Spirit dwells. Our problem is what we do with our bodies. It is a dreadful hypocrisy to have the Holy Spirit inside us, adorning us inwardly with His glory and power as His temple, yet outwardly we mingle and mix with the world through the vehicle of our bodies.

When Paul wrote the Corinthians about gluttony, sexual immorality and worldliness, he told them, "Know ye not that your bodies are the members of Christ? Shall I then take the members of Christ, and make them the members of an harlot? God forbid. What? Know ye not that he which is joined to an harlot is one body? For two, saith he, shall be one flesh. But he that is joined unto the Lord is one spirit" (1 Corinthians 6:15-17).

Then he concludes with the statement we've been examining: "Therefore glorify God in your body" (1 Corinthians 6:20).

When you gave your life to Jesus Christ and asked Him to be the Lord of your life, He did what you asked. He sent His Spirit to create you anew and to live in your heart. Now you are not your own. You gave your life to Him. Paul said that you were "bought with a price," and especially notice that you were "bought." Now you are His.

When we walk back into the world or pick up an attitude

that is so worldly we become offensive to the holiness of God, we are dragging the Holy Spirit right into the middle of an unholy situation. He never asked to be taken to these places. When we mix and mingle our bodies and minds with the world, Paul says it is the same as taking the members of Christ and uniting them to a harlot.

The day you declared Jesus Christ to be the Lord of your life, you chose to give your authority over your body, soul and spirit to Him. You are no longer in charge.

Imagine a wife saying to her husband, "I love you, and I want to stay married to you forever. But I have authority over my own body, will and emotions, and I want to have an affair with another man." This is unthinkable and completely unacceptable. How dare she violate her marriage vows in such a detestable manner and defile her covenant with her husband!

But that is too frequently what believers do to the Lord Jesus Christ. They declare their vows to Him when they call Him Lord. Then they violate their covenant with Him by re-uniting themselves with the spirit of the world.

The Holy Spirit goes where you go and sees what you see. Are you taking Him places He would never lead you?

When we understand that the Holy Spirit lives in us, it will change the way we perceive ourselves and the way we do business in life. It will change the way we talk, the way we act, the way we think and the way we behave.

What an honor to be the dwelling place of the Holy Spirit! Just think, almighty God designed for Himself a home in our hearts. What greater honor is there than this? If you need a self-image booster, stop and meditate on this. You have the riches of Jesus Christ inside you.

We must remember that we are members of Christ, and what we do to ourselves, we do to Him too. He indwells us through the person of the Holy Spirit. We must learn to honor and respect the presence of God in our lives.

Paul used this illustration to make a point. It drives the

point fairly deep — being worldly is a serious mistake for the Christian.

You were bought with a price. The Holy Spirit has fashioned you to be the highly decorated shrine of God. This work He did in you is long-lasting and permanent. He has come to dwell in you for the rest of your life. He is a permanent indweller.

TWENTY

A
DIVINE
LOVER

IN THE last chapter we looked at the word *dwelleth* in James 4:5: "The Spirit that dwelleth in us lusteth to envy." The next word we must consider is the word *lust*.

For the most part, the word *lust* has a very bad connotation in our minds. We think of sexual lust, for example, as something which must be eradicated from our lives. We think of a greedy kind of lust as an excessive desire for material possessions. Lust is something we do not want to confess proudly as a part of our lives. We want to get rid of it.

But James tells us that the Holy Spirit has lust. Because He is the Spirit of holiness (Romans 1:4), the lust of the Holy Spirit must be a healthy, godly kind of lust. This point about the lust of the Holy Spirit is so important that we must stop and see exactly what James is trying to say to us here.

The word *lusteth* is taken from the Greek word *epipothei* (ep-ee-poth-eh-ee), which is a compound of two Greek words, *epi* and *pothei*. The word *epi* means "for," and the word *pothei* means "an intense desire or yearning." Compounded together as we find them in James 4:5, they describe an intense, abnormal, excessive yearning. Usually this word is used to indicate something that is morally wrong or sinful.

For example, this word could adequately be used to picture a drug addict. Every day he needs a new fix of drugs to carry him into the next day. When the last fix wears off, and his body is desperately crying out for a new infusion of chemicals, he is nearly doubled over in pain — yearning, straining and crying out for the next injection. Everything in him is focused on getting those chemicals. He is consumed with his need for more. The word *epipothei* could describe that kind of yearning.

The word *epipothei* could also be used to describe the behavior of a sexual addict. Going from one sexual experience to the next, he is driven to keep going and going. In this case, the desire is so abnormal that enough is never enough. The desire can never be satisfied. These people are raging with lust to have more and more sexual encounters.

It is interesting that James would use the word *lust* to describe the Holy Spirit in this chapter. In verse 2 of this same chapter, James rebuked his readers for being lustful for worldly possessions. He told them, "Ye lust, and have not." But this Greek word for "lust" is different. It is the word *epithumos* (ep-ee-thoo-mos), which also describes lust, but it does not carry the same dramatic force as the word *epipothei*. The Holy Spirit's lust is stronger than the lust of our flesh, and that's good news!

Still, why would James use this word to describe the Holy Spirit? Does the Holy Spirit really have lust? The word *lust* is not bad unless it is used in a bad connotation. It can be used in a good way. James 4:5 demonstrates that by telling us the Holy Spirit "lusteth."

First Peter 1:12 also shows us that angels lust in a good way: "To them it was revealed that, not to themselves, but to us they were ministering the things which now have been reported to you through those who have preached the gospel to you by the Holy Spirit sent from heaven — things which angels desire to look into" (NKJV).

Look at the phrase "things which angels desire to look into." The word *desire* is the Greek word for *lust,* and the phrase "look into" is from the Greek word *parakupto* (pa-ra-kup-to), which means "to stretch the head forward, to look at something." *Parakupto* can best be illustrated by a young boy who wants to look over the top of a fence but can't quite reach high enough. In order to see what's on the other side of the fence, he stands high on his tiptoes and stretches upward with all of his might, until finally he is able to peek over the top to see what is on the other side.

Put all of this together, and it tells us that angels are so desirous (the Greek word for "lust") of what we experience in our salvation that they are consumed with a desire to "peek" (the Greek word *parakupto*) in on our meetings, on our jobs, on our total experience in Jesus Christ.

My point is this: The word *lust* normally denotes something that is bad, but it can also denote something that is good if it is used in a good context. When it comes to the Holy Spirit, lust is wonderful and divine.

So what does this verse mean? What is the Holy Spirit yearning for so desperately? One expositor has translated this verse to read, "The Spirit that dwelleth in us has an intense, abnormal, excessive yearning...." What does the Holy Spirit want so much that He has an abnormal desire to possess it?

The Object of the Holy Spirit's Love and Affection

After all the Holy Spirit has done in us, it should be no great shock to discover the Holy Spirit is in love with us. The fact that our mixing and mingling with the world is viewed as adultery by Him should alert us to the intense love and affection He has for us.

The Holy Spirit was sent to be our Helper and Comforter. While He does many other things, His primary job is to help us find Jesus Christ, help us grow as Christians, help us witness, help us worship, help us understand God's Word and so on.

As our indweller, our sealer, our sanctifier, our power, the source of our new life in Christ, He loves us. His work, His attention, His gifts, His power and His Word are all directed toward us. We are the object of His love and affection.

As a divine lover who lives on the inside of us, His love and affection are set single-heartedly on us. He passionately yearns to fulfill His responsibility to the Father to help, teach, guide and empower us.

James used the word *epipothei* to describe the Holy Spirit's intense desire to possess and fill us. The word *epipothei* emphatically means the Holy Spirit wants more and more of us. When it comes to you and me, He can never get enough.

At the time of this writing, I have walked with God for three decades. In these years I have learned one important thing about my relationship with God: It doesn't matter how much I surrender to His sanctifying power today, by tomorrow He will be asking me to surrender more. Every second, every minute, every hour, every day, every week, every year that passes by, my eyes are illuminated to new areas of my life which have never been surrendered, and He asks me to yield those areas to His control.

During the altar call when I was saved, the congregation was singing "I Surrender All." Ever since that time I've been surrendering all as the Holy Spirit convicts me and shows me areas I've never fully surrendered. I called Jesus "Lord" more than thirty years ago, but I am still learning to accept His Lordship in various areas of my life. It doesn't matter how much I think I've surrendered or how yielded I think I've become, there is always more to surrender and more He desires to possess of my life.

Likewise, the Holy Spirit desires to possess you — all of you — and this desire is so intense that, compared to natural, human lust, it almost appears excessive. He is focused on changing you, empowering you, conforming you to the image of Jesus Christ and helping you to fulfill God's plan for your life.

The amazing thing is that the Holy Spirit is in me and thinking of me, and He is in you and thinking of you at the same time. He concentrates on each believer, always looking for ways to help them in their spiritual journey.

The Jewish believers to whom James was writing were consumed with a lust for worldly possessions. First Peter 1:12 says the angels are consumed with desire to peek in on us to get a view of the new birth and this glorious church age. And the Holy Spirit is consumed with a flaming, always growing, passionate desire to fill us up with His love and affection.

That is why it is so hurtful to the Spirit of God when we shun Him and give our attention to other things. Hebrews 10:29 says this insensitivity insults the Holy Spirit. The verse says, "Of how much sorer punishment, suppose ye, shall he be thought worthy, who hath trodden under foot the Son of God, and hath counted the blood of the covenant, wherewith he was sanctified, an unholy thing, and hath done despite to the Spirit of grace?"

Because the Holy Spirit is called "the Spirit of grace," it tells us He will work with us a very long time before He is insulted by our behavior. Though He can be grieved, He is not easily offended and wounded. He is not that fragile.

He knows our frame and that we are dust (Psalm 103:14). His mercy is great toward those who fear Him (Psalm 103:11). As a father has compassion on his children, so the Lord has compassion on them that fear Him (Psalm 103:13).

The Spirit's grace is long-lasting and full of loving-kindness. It would take something very great to insult the Spirit whose name is grace. Yet the Bible clearly teaches that when we discount Him, ignore Him and treat His Word as unimportant in our lives, it insults the Spirit of grace.

It is almost as if the Holy Spirit says, "After all I've done for you...after I've given you My love...after I've given you the new birth...after I've sealed you...after I've sanctified you...after I've empowered you for service...after I've done all of this for you, how can you so easily turn Me off and give your body, mind and soul to other things?"

This is what grieves the Holy Spirit.

What area of your life is God dealing with you about right now? What area of your life do you need to surrender to the Holy Spirit? Is your tongue under His control? Is your thinking under His control? How are your attitudes? Are you surrendering your thought life to the Lord? How about your money? Are your spending habits and your giving under the control of the Holy Spirit?

If your answer to all of these questions is, "Yes, I'm doing all I know to do to surrender to Him," then simply wait until tomorrow. If you will allow Him to speak to your heart in your quiet time tomorrow, He will reveal another area which needs to be surrendered to His sanctifying presence.

Let Him love you! Let Him control you! Let Him exercise His authority in your life! Let Him flood you with His divine desire! Every intention He has for you is good, holy and pure. What wrong can you do by surrendering your life, your mind, your family, your spouse, your business, your ministry, your actions and your behavior to the Holy Spirit?

The Holy Spirit "dwelleth" in us, and He "lusteth" for us. Put these together, and you understand that He permanently abides within you and yearns for you.

He will never be satisfied with a shallow fellowship. He wants real communion with you. Now we must look at the third important point in this verse — the word *envy*.

TWENTY-ONE

THE DESIRE
OF THE
HOLY SPIRIT

IMAGINE THE emotions of a young man who discovers someone else has seized the heart of his sweetheart. That's the same feeling James was describing when he wrote, "The Spirit that dwelleth in us lusteth to *envy*" (James 4:5, italics added). In the last two chapters we've seen how the Holy Spirit dwells in us and longs for us. Now let's look at the extra depth of meaning the word *envy* adds to this verse.

This word comes from the Greek word *phthonos* (fthonos), which is used frequently in literature from the New

173

Testament period, so we know precisely what it means. The word *phthonos* means "jealousy, ill will or malice." This is jealousy so strong that it tends toward malice and produces envy. The young man who lost his lover feels jealous for his old relationship to be restored and most likely will bear malice in his heart toward the romantic bandit. He is envious of that relationship and wants it back.

By now James 4:5 should be clear to us. The Holy Spirit is a lover. He is preoccupied with us. He wants to possess us totally and desires that our affection also be set on Him. When we walk and talk like unbelievers and give our lives to other things, He feels like a lover who has been robbed. He feels jealous for His relationship with us to be restored. He has divine malice for the worldliness that has usurped His role in our lives. And He is filled with envy to see things put back the way they should be.

When you put all three words — *dwelleth, lusteth* and *envy* — together, this paints quite a picture. The Holy Spirit is not a passive partner. He aggressively and actively pursues you and me. He fiercely wants more of me and more of you. When we give a piece of ourselves to something or someone else's control, He wants to seize it and bring it back under His divine control. He even has malice toward our preoccupation with other things.

We live in the world, work in the world and function as human beings in the world. There is no way to get around that. Jesus didn't pray that we would be removed from the world but that we would be *kept* from the world (John 17:15).

There is nothing wrong with going to work, buying a house, purchasing a new car or liking beautiful clothes. Those things are great and very needful in this world. They are not wrong unless they consume and preoccupy our thoughts.

Let's not forget the fact that all kinds of things can preoccupy our thinking. Even your ministry can so preoccupy your thoughts that you never think of the Holy Spirit or your relationship with Him. Yes, that seems like a contradiction, but it is very possible to be so involved in good works that we never spend time with the Lord, read His Word or listen to what His Spirit wants to say to our hearts.

Sometimes it is just the cares of this life that pull us away from the Holy Spirit. We can get so busy, so committed to do so many things, that it deteriorates our spiritual life. Amazing as it is, even good things or things that are neutral — if taken to an extreme — become adulterous in the eyes of the Lord.

Only the Lord knows how to balance us, and the only way He can speak to us and keep us in balance is if we open our hearts and spiritual ears to hear Him. That won't happen if we aren't setting aside a special time to spend with Him every day.

Where is your mind most of the time? In the garage? On your boat? In your kitchen? In your yard? On your job? On redecorating your house? At the movies? Where are your thoughts? The answer to that question will probably tell you what consumes you most in life.

You can work in your profession without losing your deep affection and sensitivity to the Holy Spirit. Don't lie to yourself and say you can't, because *you know you can.*

You can be a wife and a good, dedicated mother and grow in your relationship with the Holy Spirit simultaneously. *You know you can.*

Don't tell yourself you have too much to do and can't spend time with the Lord. You basically do what you want to do. If having communion with the Holy Spirit is a priority, you'll make time for Him. If communion with Him is not a priority of yours, then you won't. It's that simple.

You could translate James 4:5 to say, "The Spirit that has come to settle down, make His home and permanently dwell in us, is bent with an all-consuming, ever-growing, excessive, passionate desire to possess us, and is envious and filled with malice toward anything or anyone who tries to take His place in our lives."

I think that says it all.

How to Make Your Heart Right With the Holy Spirit

Perhaps you're reading this book and thinking, "I've got so much to learn about the Holy Spirit. I didn't know I was supposed to have communion with Him. I didn't know that I could learn to depend upon Him as my Comforter. I didn't know I could grieve Him with my attitudes. I didn't realize how important our relationship is."

If that is you, then you're in a great place today. You are standing at the threshold of a whole new realm of God in your life. For you right now, humility is the name of the game. That is why James tells us, "But he giveth more grace. Wherefore he saith, God resisteth the proud, but giveth grace unto the humble...Draw nigh to God, and he will draw nigh to you" (James 4:6,8).

The proud believer who refuses to listen and come back to God will have a rocky road ahead. As we have learned in chapter 18, God opposes the worldly Christian. For the worldly Christian, there is nothing but frustration in the future. God will block his way in order to frustrate him and bring him back to his senses. Though it eventually brings forth much fruit, this is a hard and painful way to grow in the Lord.

But God gives "grace unto the humble." The word *humble* in Greek is the word *tapeinos* (tap-i-nos), and it describes those who are lowly and humble of mind. This is the very opposite of the person who is haughty, self-reliant, independent and unrepentant. The humble person is lowly, needy and willing to receive correction and change. God's grace flows freely to the person with this right attitude.

Furthermore, James promises that if we draw closer to God, He will draw closer us. God and a repentant heart attract each other just as two magnets are drawn together. As the humble Christian recognizes the need to change and draws closer to the Lord, the Lord Himself comes closer to that person.

The Spirit comes to stay once He indwells the heart. We do not "draw nigh" to have the Holy Spirit. We already have Him inside of us. This drawing nigh to the Lord is our first step toward entering into communion with Him through the Holy Spirit.

I can't help but wonder how many Christians will die, go to heaven and find out all they missed because they never experienced the communion of the Holy Spirit.

Don't let that be your story!

The apostle Paul prayed, "The grace of the Lord Jesus Christ, and the love of God, and the communion of the Holy Spirit be with you all. Amen" (2 Corinthians 13:14, NKJV).

That "amen" in Greek means "so be it!" Paul was not just praying a sweet-sounding prayer to be stuck at the end of an epistle. He really meant what he prayed. Thus, he concluded by saying, "Amen! So be it."

Likewise, my prayer for you is that your spirit is stirred to move upward in your relationship with God, that you will come to know the intimacy, the partnership and the responsibility of the Holy Spirit in your life.

This is the secret place in God that I first began to discover in 1974 as a result of attending that Kathryn Kuhlman miracle service on the campus of Oral Roberts University.

Just as I can look back and say that was my starting place for a new and wonderful relationship with the Spirit of God, I pray that this book will be your starting place.

Amen! So be it done in your life!

> The grace of the Lord Jesus Christ, and the love of God, and the communion of the Holy Spirit be with you all (1 Corinthians 13:14, NKJV).

Barclay, William. *New Testament Words*. Belleville, Mich.: Westminster Press, 1976.

Berry, George Ricker. *The Interlinear Greek-English New Testament*. Hinds & Nobel, 1897. Grand Rapids, Mich.: Baker Book House/Revell, 1977.

Brown, Colin. *New International Dictionary of New Testament Theology*. Grand Rapids, Mich.: Zondervan, 1986.

Clark, Walter Jerry. *How to Use New Testament Greek Study Aids*. Neptune, N.J.: Loizeaux Brothers, 1984.

Kittel, Gephard. *Theological Dictionary of the New Testament*. Grand Rapids, Mich.: Wm. B. Eerdmans, 1976.

Perschbacher, Wesley. *The New Analytical Greek Lexicon*. Peabody, Mass.: Hendrickson Publishers, 1990.

Rienecker, Fritz and Cleon Rogers. *The Linguistic Key to the Greek New Testament*. Grand Rapids, Mich.: Zondervan, 1982.

Strong, James. *The New Strong's Exhaustive Concordance of the Bible*. Nashville, Tenn.: Thomas Nelson, 1984.

Thayer, Joseph. *Greek-English Lexicon of the New Testament: Numerically Coded to Strong's Exhaustive Concordance*. Grand Rapids, Mich.: Baker Book House/Revell, 1988.

Trench, R. C. *Trench's Synonyms of the New Testament*. Grand Rapids, Mich.: Baker Book House/Revell, 1989.

Wigram, George. *The Englishman's Greek Concordance of the New Testament*. Grand Rapids, Mich.: Baker Book House/Revell, 1984.

Wuest, Kenneth. *Word Studies in the Greek New Testament*. Grand Rapids, Mich.: Wm. B. Eerdmans, 1969.

Raised as a Southern Baptist, Rick Renner enjoyed great biblical instruction, but he saw little of the power of God. After he was baptized in the Spirit as a young teen, he knew the power of God but seldom found scriptural teaching when he went to charismatic meetings.

The cry of his heart today is to see the reality of the Word and the power of the Holy Spirit come together in the lives of believers.

Renner prepared for ministry by studying Greek and journalism at the University of Oklahoma, where he met his wife, Denise. He pastored at several churches before entering the teaching ministry full-time.

In 1991 God directed Renner to relocate to Jelgava, Latvia, with his wife and three sons. At first he taught a Bible school and held crusades throughout the region. But soon the Holy Spirit prompted him to start a television program as well. The result was "Good News With Rick Renner," which reaches millions of people.

In 1993 Renner established the Good News Church, and in 1994 he founded a Bible school to train pastors and workers for all the churches that were springing up because of the revival taking place in Russia and the surrounding republics.

Although he lives in Latvia, Renner continues to minister regularly in America and Europe, and he maintains offices in Tulsa, Oklahoma. He has written several books, including Dream Thieves, Dressed to Kill, Living in the Combat Zone and Spiritual Weapons to Defeat the Enemy.

For more information about his ministry, contact:

Rick Renner Ministries
P.O. Box 47228
Tulsa, OK 74147
(918) 496-3213